LIBIDO

Studies in Phenomenology and Existential Philosophy

Temple of Konarak. *Courtesy of the Archaeological Survey of India.*

LIBIDO

The French Existential Theories

Alphonso Lingis

Indiana University Press
Bloomington

Manufactured in the United States of America

Library of Congress Cataloging in Publication Data

Lingis, Alphonso, 1933–
    Libido: the French existential theories.

    (Studies in phenomenology and existential
philosophy)
    Bibliography: p.
    Includes index.
    1. Phenomenology. 2. Sex. 3. Philosophy, French—
20th century. I. Title. II. Series.
B829.5.L54   1985   128'.3   84-48483
ISBN 0-253-33415-2
    1 2 3 4 5   89 88 87 86 85

Contents

Preface

What is the languor, the torpor that weighs on the body libidinally aroused; what is the unconsciousness that darkens the mind preoccupied with erotic affairs? What are kisses, caresses, embraces aiming to do, to effect, to communicate, to discover, or to dissimulate? One is never so exposed, so vulnerable as when erotically obsessed, Freud remarked; what is this will to weakness, to debility, to dismemberment we call *libido*? What is the relationship between the inner vital functions—respiration, digestion, coordination, and locomotion—and the surface effects—heraldic patterns on the toucan's beak, glyphs on the zebra, erotogenic surface? What is it about the orifices of our bodies that make them so charged for the eye and the touch? What it is about what Michaelangelo could only see as repulsive ugliness of the genital organs that so excites the cerebral processes? Socrates's Diotima, in Plato's *Symposium*, argued that all eros craves only beauty and immortality, immortal beauty, the splendor of eternity; how is it then that Aschenbach in Venice is more interesting—not merely intellectually interesting, but *troubling*—than Tadzio? Is it not the mortal flesh and blood we love that makes us forget all the beautiful and immortal causes? What is the languor, the vulnerability of the erotically denuded one that incites this—and every—profanation? What governs the flux and reflux of tension and of susceptibility in the carnal substance? What is the gratification in the tormented pleasures of voluptuousness, never contented? Why is the lustful interrogation which something in us addresses to every man and woman that passes not silenced as we enter into more and more lucid agreements, collaborations, conversations, institutions? The language of the libido is unconscious, the unconsciousness a lascivious murmur which accompanies all our avowed messages. What is its code, its grammar, its syntax; what are its categories, its rhetoric, its answers?

And what could *philosophy* answer? What could a philosophy of libido be, if not some moralizing and ascetic commentaries on the generalizations of empirical biology and psychology?

The father of philosophy imagined that philosophical dialectics alone could exhibit the true finality of the libidinal impulses; it would do so by bringing to light its own finality. In the *Symposium*, Socrates's discourse taught that the philosophic craving to contemplate the pure forms and the order of the universe is erotic; it is the longing that troubled infantile carnal curiosity long before there could be any question of genital coupling. In humans sexuality does not simply maintain the species; it is the locus of a metaphysical finality. Strange doctrine! The human species, unseasonal, the most sexed, is afflicted with a sexuality that is not for the sake of the maintenance of the species, nor for the sake of the pleasure of the individual. A teaching Socrates puts into the mouth of a priestess or oracle.

And then—two thousand five hundred years of philosophical silence on the matter. Yet philosophical concepts forged in antiquity, the concepts of matter, objectivity, cause, and telos, did function as the framework within which empirical sciences assembled and organized their observations. The very concept of the body objectively considered is the heir of the Platonic conceptual system in which body and mind, fact and value, material and formal, were first distinguished.

In recent years, in France, sexuality suddenly became again a central issue in philosophy. This book shall study how this happened and what it yielded in six major authors—Jean-Paul Sartre, Maurice Merleau-Ponty, Emmanuel Levinas, Jean-François Lyotard, Gilles Deleuze, and Félix Guattari.

Phenomenology was originally a program aiming to identify the fundamental evidences of our sciences in neutral descriptions; it required a suspension of metaphysical commitments as to the ultimate reality of the phenomena to be described. It could be useful to exhibit thus the basic phenomena of our experiences of ourselves also, and of our bodies. These are heterogeneous—the objective body, given in controlled chemical, physical, electrical, mechanical observations, can be distinguished from the body as it appears to the one who activates it, who is walking, laboring, caressing; the body that feels does not perceive itself in the form it presents to the onlooker. Phenomenology's metaphysical neutralism first prescribes elaborating a pure description of each of these distinct phenomena of our corporeality, and correlating them with the observational procedures, the subjective attitudes, to which they are given, and treating them as all epistemologically equivalent. Yet the metaphysical neutralism is provisional; the perception by an outside observer of my body is a perception I perceive (I hear or read the linguistic signs with which he communicates it to me); it does not prevail over my perception of myself. The selective or abstractive perception of scientific observation comes after the concrete natural perception, the theoretical formulation comes after the sensible perception. The upshot is that the objective representation of our bodies is not alone to have validity; it in fact presupposes the validity of other presentations of our bodies.

These epistemological considerations justified a systematic effort to inventory the multiple phenomena of our corporeality—among them, the erotic figure of our body, that given in libidinal experience. When we walk we certainly have a sense of where our limbs and torso are and how they look, but this perception is not that of an anatomy diagram; likewise, erotic behavior addresses itself to, and can be understood only in terms of, a specifically carnal apparition of a body. The empiricist project of understanding physiology on the basis of anatomy, of extending one analysis of a material position or a movement to all kinds of movements our bodies make, had incorporated an uncriticized epistemological bias for a certain kind of objectivity.

The task was clear—describe rigorously the traits that make a body appear erotic, describe the erotic organization of its perceptible phenomena. The body as a spectacle for theoretical observation does not stand and conduct itself as does the body mobilized for collaboration, nor the efficacious body as does the orgasmic body; describe then the carnal form and properties. The task turned out to be more difficult than it first seemed. The six major authors this book examines have formulated their accounts of the libidinal body, the carnal, in very different ways.

Erotic behavior is both the stand and the conduct by which a body becomes orgasmic, presents itself as an erotic object—

and the responses it calls for and induces in the body that witnesses it. What is distinctive of kisses, caresses, embraces, copulations, as behaviors? What are they addressed to, what provokes them, how do they differ from gestures, expressions, and actions, what finalities might they have? Analysis of their anatomical substrates will not answer these questions, any more than the anatomical investigation of the mouth and throat explains what speech is. Phenomenology should impose rigor in the description; it is in fact more difficult than one thinks to avoid importing metaphysical commitments and epistemological evaluations with the terms one uses. A philosophical consciousness trained to recognize them can be of real help even to the scientific consciousness disciplined to restrict the meaning of its terms to the usages fixed in explicit definitions.

Erotic behavior is not simply commotion in one's anatomy; it is a way of relating with others. Just what is the alterity that is addressed in this way? Just what does one strive to become present to through kisses and orgasms? The word *metaphysics*, we know, got its use through a misunderstanding: originally merely labelling the writings "after" those on "physics" in the Aristotelian corpus, it came to mean the discourse concerning what is beyond the physical, beyond the perceptually given or empirically observable. Levinas uses this old term to designate primarily *the other*—all speech is a movement on my part to reach what is definitively other than me, unrepresentable by me, unconvertible into my experience. The other would be the topic of metaphysical consideration. In our erotic relationships are we not seeking a sense or a presence of the other beyond what one makes contact with in the exchange systems of discourse, productive labor, commerce, and the institutions of the polis—and which are systems in which I and the other are taken to be, or are made, interchangeable?

The phenomenological ideal would be to put in the terms of its description the very meaning conveyed in the phenomena themselves. Phenomenology presupposes that the theoretical activity follows a multitude of pretheoretical activities which also make sense, that is, constitute meaning in the succession of their own movements and in the configurations of their fields of operation. Does the sense of erotic movements and moments link up to form a discourse or the plot of a history? What is the erotic sense and how does it differ from a conceptual meaning? How are erotic movements coded? What grammar, what syntax, what logic is there in the tale our erotic lives tell?

The phenomenological project, so clear when first launched, turned out to harbor ambiguities and lead to strange convictions. The six major authors we are here considering are writers of quite exceptional perspicacity and linguistic skill; their ingeniousness not only at describing the ordinary facts of eroticism but at discerning details, complications, conflicts not before formulated in all the literature on eroticism in our culture is remarkable. In assessing the work of these six authors, work elaborated over a forty-year period, we not only will see a very rich accumulation of finely delineated observations; we will also study the difficulties the phenomenological enterprise encountered and the transformations it underwent. The idea of what the libido is varies remarkably with each author; the idea of what erotic sense could be and how it might be formulated in the neutral language of description, are very different. The very idea of metaphysic-free, presupposition-free description of phenomena changes. This movement of research can then be seen to be by no means at its term. It has by no means exhausted the inventory of phenomena to be recorded and elucidated; its own procedures and aims remain in question. Our study makes an argument out of the succession of books it examines. It concludes with an assessment of the argument—a formulation of how the libidinal body can now be characterized, what the libidinal drive is, what the erotic sense is, and what alterity commands in the erotic imperative.

Around these six philosophers, and to a very large measure incited by them, there has been produced a huge body of psychological work, investigating cases, exploring correlations, and extending the essential insights of the phenomenological account of the basic structures of sexuality into the domains of psychopathology. There is also a very large body of therapeutic literature. Our book restricts its aim to elucidating the essential philosophical positions that have made this psychological and psychotherapeutic work possible.

Grateful acknowledgment is made of the Humanities Research Fund of the Pennsylvania State University for generous material support of this project.

And warm thanks to Professor David Krell, of the University of Essex, for so much help in the composition of the manuscript.

LIBIDO

1.

Freedom and Slavery in Sexuality

Sexuality is the passion of one body for another. The violence of sexual pleasure is the result of our total investment in this opaque sensuous entangling—our investment, Sartre will say, of what is most abstract, most human, the pure transparent longing for freedom, the risk of enslavement, the desire to enslave.

What, then, does it mean for us to *be corporeal?*

Philosophy has consecrated certain categories with which to conceptualize corporeality: the category of matter, correlate of that of form, composing together the ancient notion of the life-principle as a force giving determination to a pure determinable; the category of mechanism, which served as the basis of the modern effort to understand the self-determining movement of an organism not in terms of an internal motor principle, but in terms of the universal principles of dynamics. These categories integrate the understanding of the nature and operation of the human body into the theory of bodies in general. As an object, a living body is to be determined by the universal characteristics of objective reality.

Here lies a first ontological error Sartre means to expose through phenomenological analysis. When we scrutinize the phenomena without ontological preconceptions, we shall find that one's own body appears in perception (that "primordial dator intuition") not really integrated into the objective world. My own body cannot form an object before me: I cannot maintain it fixed while I take different perspectival viewpoints on

1

it; I cannot, strictly speaking, *observe* it. Yet this cannot mean that the experience I have of my own body is fallacious or illusory; I do act effectively in the world of objects with it. The phenomenal appearance of my-body-for-me has to be described, without correcting it with data taken from the way my body appears to others (and the way the bodies of others appear to me). Then one will see that the problem of understanding the relations between body and mind has been made irresolvable because the properties defining mind were derived from one's experience of one's own mind, but the properties defining body were derived from perception of the bodies of others.

It is the bodies of others that appear as objects of perception, action, and feeling. But their objectivity is distinctive—they take form in perceptual experiences different from those in which inorganic objects are given. They form sensible figures holding a posture and turning toward exterior and even absent coordinates. A living body and a dummy are perceived differently. The perceiving of another's body and the perceiving of an inanimate object are as different and even mutually exclusive as are the perceiving of a real thing and the imagining of an unreal phantasm.

In addition, my body appears to others as a phenomenon like those in which their bodies appear to me, and I am myself somehow aware of the way my incorporated existence appears to them. This, my-body-for-others as I sense it, constitutes a third series of phenomena of corporeality.

To understand our corporeality, the first task is to determine the characteristics of these different series of phenomena—those my own corporeal side shows me, those in which others appear as bodies to me, and those that give me a sense of the body they take me to be.

1. *My Own Body for Me*

What is perceived is not perceived *in* one's corporeal substance nor *through* it. Just how does my own body figure in my field of perception?

Sensible perception is a presentation of a field of patterns in exteriority. A clearing opens, a zone of transparency, a "pool of nothingness," about which separation, distinction, exposition is possible, about which a field of colors, shapes, lights, and shadows takes form, before which a figure separates from a background. The phosphorescent faces of things are not simply drifting; they take their places in a certain order. When the field shifts, it shifts in a systematic way; perspectival lines control the sizes and shapes of the forms and the ways that forms eclipse one another.

The spread of forms, right and left, upwards and downwards, specifies a reference point; the approach and departure of tones indicate a center; the articulation of textures and the amassing of substances, and their disarticulation in depth and in distance, fixes a focal point. This center is the anchorage of the sensibility; it is an ever-present "here" about which the paths of the visible spread, to which the sounds approach and from which they recede, where the wave-front of things becomes pressure and density. The focal point where all the lines of perspective converge is part of the visual field but is not itself a visual object. Pure point of departure, pure here-from-which, never taking form as an object before the sensibility, it is the way my sensibility is fixed in its field of objects.

The field does not consist of a system of forms simply juxtaposed; the forms are dynamically connected. They interlock, turn one another, form paths and instrumental chains, means-ends systems—for an agency which is oneself. The direction outward of means toward ends designates retrospectively a center of thrust. This center functions instrumentally but is not in its turn activated instrumentally. One is not manipulating one's own hand with anything. It is the point of departure of one's forces in the field of masses and resistances. It is the way my agency is fixed in the field of implements.

Affective tonalities saturate the forms and the layout of things. Not one color is visible without being restful, agitating, serene, gay, or dismal; not one sound is audible that is not melancholy, brash, or buoyant. Forms are imposing, quaint, squat; horizons bleak, desolate, majestic. These tonalities emerge by contrast with one another, and by contrast with the core they affect, about which they spread. The core is not another affectively charged object, but a neutral level with which all the affective tonalities of the field contrast. This core, neither alluring nor repellent—stale or neutral for itself—functions as the insertion of my feeling in the field of the felt.

If my body does not appear to me as a perceptible, manipulable, affecting object, that is not because my own perception of myself would be fallacious or illusory—"subjective"; it is because my corporeality functions in the ordered field of perception, action, and feeling as point of departure, here-from-which—the surpassed or past. It is the core of darkness, the hollow behind the instrumental layout, the neutral level which every perceiving, acting, and feeling intention quits.

2. The Subjectivity and the Objectification of Others

If my body ever can be an object, it will be so for others; and the properties of this object can only be divined from the attitudes they take toward it. In the classical discussions of the problem of other minds, the object-appearances of the others' bodies were taken as given, and their subjectivity was taken as something only deduced, on the basis of the analogy between my own body and theirs. For Sartre, my own objectivity is for me something only surmised. From what? From the attitudes, that is, the subjectivity, of the others, which is immediately given and not deduced from their object-appearances.

A direct experience of alien subjectivity means an experience of the other as a power to see, a force of love or desire or hatred, a sovereignty that judges and orders, an efficacious agency. Such a being is encountered in my experience of being objectified—being seen, being wanted or despised, being judged, manipulated, being impotent and acted upon. With Sartre, for whom freedom is the determining characteristic of subjectivity, this is the compelling experience of the force of an alien freedom. It is experienced in my enslavement.

The impact of the encounter with another occurs as a structure of fear, shame, and pride, rather than a structure of perception or interaction. This is proper to the Sartrean explanation—and gives an essentially dramatic character to human coexistence in his analyses.

The sense of one's own freedom is *anxiety*. Every move of subjectivity is an option and a determination, both of its object and of itself. But subjectivity cannot be a disengaging of things without freeing itself from being. This is what one senses in anxiety—that one is not bound or held even by one's own determinations. The one who finds himself on a cliffside path where rocks have fallen senses the instability of the world which must support him from the inner tonality of *fear.* If he is to get across alive, he must count on his own perceptions and forces to deal with the possibilities of support to be found in the obstructed path. But his eyes scan the void below, and the possibility, and temptation, to escape fear by suicide presents itself. The *anxiety* that now arises is the sense that he cannot count on himself either, on his determination to hold to a certain form of behavior. The determination he has had the power to give himself is already past, and has lost its force not because it has passed away, but just because it has come to pass, come to be—and subjectivity's freedom consists in an active withdrawal from all being. Anxiety is the form this insight into the nature of one's own subjectivity takes.

It is *abject or defiant fear* that touches directly the core essence of alien subjectivity. That I am seen comes as the sense of being vulnerable, exposed, prey to alien powers; to be seen is to be foreseeable. My size and stature, which had spread out my powers and applied them to the front-line instrumentalities, now become the outspread surface of my vulnerability. I feel myself held in what I took to be an instrumental field at my service. I now sense my own powers only in and through the other; it is his look, sweeping over the field with tense movements, which shows me that to him I am not what I seem to be—am not to be trusted, am one who could try to hide, escape, or attack—and indicates to me these possibilities as my power.

The inward sense of being exposed is something immediately certain; my uneasiness cleaves to me. Yet precisely how my forces look to the gaze to which they are exposed, and exactly what instrumentalities the things about me present to an alien intention, elude me. The tonality of fear, that shifting inner malaise, reflects the indeterminateness of the power it senses—an alien freedom.

This fear is essentially abject; it is shame. For what I am afraid of is not so much the other's strength as his judgment—or his strength at the service of his judgment. Like Nietzsche, Sartre thinks that the essential power that is in man is his power to evaluate. To feel my subjectivity subjected to alien judgment is to discover an essential degradation of my being which was existing only for itself; my existence has become *for-others*, my subjectivity a subjection. Shame has its own cognitive value and its own kind of certainty. It reveals the obtrusiveness I am, the object-obstacle I am, with a compelling force I could not doubt; my shame is a confession. The pride and glory I can derive from the place I occupy in the worlds of others—from the discovery of multiple worlds outside the one that opens about me, and from my own multiplication, my turning up, a fascinating or repelling object, in all of them—is derivative of this fundamental abjection.

Alien subjectivity is something encountered. Where, and when, is it? The other's look cannot be perceived on his eyes; the subjectivity, the judgment, in his force cannot be apprehended. It is everywhere *on me*, in the object I have become. And the alien look catches me up with my environment; its power takes hold of my instrumental systems and gears them together with an inverse finality. The other is not separated from me as an object is separated, by a distance in which other objects are or can be inserted; he is separated by his being *other than* what I can situate in my setting.

And he is outside of what I can make or keep present. Others keep hold of bits of my past which I surrendered long ago; others, like the God of Molinism, are able to foresee what I will freely determine myself to do, something I myself cannot know. The other is not contained in the present at which my life keeps itself stationed; he and I are never contemporary.

The one that looks at me is individual, with an individuality that does not take shape as an instantiation of a class or of a general form. One cannot argue here that for this entity to be apprehended there must first have been in my structure an advance-hold on the dimension of possibility that the empirical encounter actualizes—for the one that comes is encountered, neither apprehended nor comprehended, not received but negating me, alterity which I do not apprehend but am apprehensive of. But the exposure I suffer, the objectivity he really effects, exposes me to all real and possible others. All possible subjectivity condemns me in the look of a solitary supplicant; my shame before humanity is not additively constituted when a second, then a third beggar looks at me with

eyes that lay claim on me. When I have fled the one who saw
me peering through the keyhole and have lost him in the
street, I continue to feel shame, I am ashamed before anyone,
feeling shame even in the midst of animals. To exist in a world
where there are other subjects is to have to justify one's existence. To know the alterity of the other—the freedom in
another—is to know shame.

Two distinctive theses frame Sartre's conception of the
other as an *object* in my experience. The first is that the sense
of the other as an object follows upon and is dependent on the
sense of the other as a free and sovereign subjectivity. It is
produced by an objectification of the other, motivated by the
affective character of the encounter with alien subjectivity. If I
suppose that that colored shape is in fact not "a hat and cloak
covering an automaton pushed by springs," it is because I have
already had the experience of being looked at. The apprehension of another subjectivity is an abject or proud apprehensiveness; objectification is a defense. This ob-ject, this form set
before oneself which keeps its distance from oneself, keeps the
subjectivity of the other at a distance.

The project of subjugation of the alien subjectivity is already contained in the structure of my shame. The feeling of
vulnerability involves a sense of concern for this being I have
to attend to; the feeling of mortification involves a sense of
having to answer for this being I am. There is an affirmation of
subjectivity in the very avowal of abject objectivity; there is
pride in this shame. Shame is both an admission of subjection,
of the right of the other to make demands on me, to question
me, to sanction or censure my being—and a concern for and
defense of that being.

Sizing up the other—*Who are you anyhow? What are you
doing in this hallway, at this hour of the night?*—I am seeking
grounds, justification, for the judgment borne upon me, situating my judge, already making him an object of my judgment. I
am locating him, surveying the correlates of his power and
envisaging his potential initiatives, which, themselves determined, limited, are already exposed to counter-initiatives on
my part; I am foreseeing his future. This locating and this
foreseeing is *perceiving somebody.*

The perception of the bodies of others is a special kind of

perception; this is the second Sartrean thesis. Such perception is, Sartre says, as different from the perception of inanimate objects, and of corpses, as perception itself is different from imagination. "When I see a rat running or an arm rising, I know beforehand where they are going, or, at least, I know they are going somewhere. Somewhere space empties itself and awaits them; around them space is full of anticipations, of natural places, and each of these places is a stopping place, a resting-place, the end of a journey."[1] The body-running is a body-perceiving—a perceiving now become a perceptible body. For me to see another's perception is to see his position as a posture polarized toward certain other objects about him that are turning to him faces they do not turn to me. For Sartre this is not, as for Husserl and Heidegger, a perceptual experience structured sympathetically or substitutively, a perception that projects itself into the place of what is perceived, to envisage a radius of the landscape as it would take form if one stood there oneself where the other is standing. For Sartre the sense that a sector of the landscape spread out in my perceptual field turns unperceived faces to another is not given in a virtual perception, nor understood, but felt. The feeling is antipathetic and not sympathetic. The other's sight is divined as an absence, a negentity, which makes its presence felt by making absences occur in the things that are turned to me—I feel their substances and forces eluding me. (I first feel my own substance and force delivered over to his power.) To objectify that sight is to locate the eyes as the center of the hemorrhage in my world. The arm-rising, the body-running arise as configurations while space empties about them. I then see a structure not visibly being propped up or driven by anything other than itself, a structure that seems to hold itself up by its inner axes of tension and to steer itself in view of objectives whose substance drains from me and draws him. To view him thus is to see that I can manipulate him—by manipulating the field so as to intercept or divert the flow of its forces toward him.

It is the force of fear that has objectified the other, and in the positions and displacements of this object my shame and my pride and my sexual desire read off alien feelings. What are seen to be emotional attitudes and moves have a distinctive structure and pacing, unlike those termed unemotional, cold, rational, pragmatic. Emotional behaviors do not apply themselves to details in their utilitarian order, but to the total layout; they attempt to alter its general articulation by abruptly changing one's whole position with regard to it. They are incantatory and magical. These attitudes and movements are not observed as expressions of a surmised immanent feeling tone, but are seen comprehensively in terms of their mundane correlates, the dangerous, repellent, or attractive field whose affective charge one oneself feels.

I perceive also, in his hands, his eyes, his chin, the love and contempt the other bears toward me. It is love and contempt I respond to in massive and incantatory ways. Though it is not impossible to maintain a determinist view of the interpsychic world and to construct rational superstructures over this network of magical interactions, such superstructures are ephemeral and unstable, collapsing when the sight of faces, postures, and gestures becomes too strong. "Man is always a sorcerer for man, and the social world is from the first magical."[2]

3. The Antinomies of Alterity

The other is encountered in an incessant alternation of subjectivity and objectivity. Each mode of the other is adequate unto itself and total. The other's subjectivity when present is totally present, his perceiving, evaluating, practical faculties implicated in my shameful apprehensiveness of his freedom. And no corner of my world is safe from him; all possibilities within my reach are open to him too. Yet an object, too, to be real, must sustain relationships with every other possible object in the field of objectivity; it must fit in, as a relay point or an obstacle, in the dynamic structure of the world—or it remains but imaginary. If the other is objectified, he is completely objectified, and all his properties are objective. His transcendence is contained in movements and attitudes of a body visibly polarized in function of their perceivable objectives; his freedom is observable as the groping manner of those movements.

These two different experiences of the other are mutually incompatible structures of the whole field of experience. They exclude one another, Sartre says, to the point that the one apparition is not perceptible in nor even conceivable from the phenomenal structure of the other.[3] Sartre's basic conviction about the comprehensive unity of the comprehending consciousness requires that this be so. Consciousness, as unlimited self-transcending and universal synthesizing, extends one perspective, one type of organization, across all being in each experience; consciousness is always being-in-the-*world*. This relationship with the whole of being is in fact what had compelled Sartre's ontological definition of consciousness as utter nonbeing.

Certainly this conception produces aporias. How, in the midst of the one experience, could the possibility of overcoming it in another experience arise? If one modality appears by disappearance of the other, how can the one be recognized to be the defeat of the other? Why do I look at a body, an object of perception, as something I have to contend with when I suddenly feel myself dangling on the end of an alien look? And what is it about the objectified body that makes it seem "an explosive instrument which I handle with care because I foresee about it the permanent possibility that *one* is going to make it explode and that with this explosion I shall suddenly experience the flight of the world from me and the alienation of my being"?[4] The look that comes to me comes from somewhere; it is not a medium in which I find myself steeped. It is no more an unsituated vision that my own can be. It is true that looking hard at his eyes, I would see only opaque membrane and blood vessels, from which it is inconceivable that there could have come that terrible judgment I felt penetrating to the core of my being. Touching the skin and feeling the pulp and bones of another's hand I no longer understand the approbation or consolation I felt from his touch. Yet, somehow, it passed there.

The perception of another as an object is not simply motivated by the objectifying perception of the inanimate setting; it is a distinct type of perception, intended to suppress the apprehensiveness that knew alien subjectivity. Yet it refers to that subjectivity as its motivation. Conversely, the experience of alien subjectivity could not turn into a project of objectifying the other unless the possibility of being located and foreseen were already latent in the elusiveness of the alien, unless this vulnerability were detected in that sovereignty. These structures which exclude one another also refer to one another. Subjectivity and objectivity are appearances *of* the other.

Yet the objection that we could not experience the other objectified as an objectification of that alien subjectivity which first threatened, that we could not taste the sense of this victory, unless "the other" were an identity under which both aspects could be subsumed, is perhaps not a compelling objection. Merleau-Ponty, who declares incomprehensible Sartre's position that subjectivity and objectivity are reciprocally incompatible in the phenomenal experience of the other, himself several times formulates the doubt as to whether I have a genuine concept of the other.[5] Is there indeed, in the subjective force that overwhelms me and turns me inside out, and in that objectified structure I hold outside myself, some essence, some invariant, that functions as an identity term for identifying them as phenomenal *Abschattungen*, profiles, of one and the same person? Is "the other" really conceived or conceivable—is it not rather the very sense of the elusive?

For Sartre "the other" is not an identity apprehended, but what one is exposed to and apprehensive of. Alterity is perceived in the subjectivity and in the objectivity that confront me each so totally as the reference by which each refers to the other by being its polar opposite. These two radically different phenomena reveal the other not to a synthesizing memory that retains a common identity in each but to a memory that recalls and divines the reversal of the one into the other.

The alternation of the two incompatible experiences of the other produces an irreducible conflict within myself. When the other turns up in my world, I find myself afflicted with an objective status. At the always surpassed, already past point of departure of my vision and my force there is an object I cannot see, an implement or obstacle I cannot manipulate, an affective charge I cannot feel. Under the other's look I find myself backed up against this object. It is my own existence as a charge, a burden. To be afraid of the other's sovereign freedom is to be afraid for this object, exposed and vulnerable in the midst of objectivity. It is not only specific characteristics of this object-side to myself, but objectivity itself that I am ashamed of; it can be for me only a degradation, a sense of my powers anticipated, my freedom trapped, my sovereignty situated and judged.

This objective being is also that of which I myself am, and of which alone I can be, proud. Enter alien subjectivity, and the world whose center I monopolized is multiplied to un-numbered versions—and I turn up in all of them. Pride is the sense of counting, having weight, turning up in the worlds of others as a force that attracts their subjectivity and absorbs it in itself.

To be an object is a value for me. My subjectivity always wanted to be something. It can continue to be conscious of the world and of itself only by continually separating itself from what is and from what it is. But being was always what it pursued, being was value itself. Objectification is fixation in being. Before the eyes of another, what I am, what I am no longer, and what I am seeking to be are integrated in his judg-ment; my life contracts into one itinerary. The core of darkness I was in the heart of the luminous world, the agitation that could be itself only by ceaselessly withdrawing from whatever is and that could prolong itself only by withdrawing from whatever it itself is, now takes form in the world as a figure indefinitely observable, whose movements are as patent and palpable as the movements of the material inertia they pit themselves against.

For Sartre the Absolute is not the kind of being subjects have—a being that flees itself and seeks itself—but a being that is given, without causes or principles and without poten-tialities or relationships. What else is this but the empiricist concept of what the objectivity of objects consists in? The being of what is taken as given is the basis and starting point of all cognitive operations; the classes, structures, and relation-ships posited by cognitive operations are derivative of the givenness of facts and owe all their validity to their power to collect and present the given. And the original being of the brute given is what gives its relative and derivative value to the being of consciousness. Being and value, the beginning and the end, coincide. Sartre takes this to mean, ontologically, that consciousness aims at objects—aims to bring out their being, but also aims to have their kind of being. Consciousness aims always at being in itself—as what it itself aims to be.

Thus the object-being I become under an alien look is also the sole object of pride; it is the sense of having become something—and one can only want to be being. It is my constitutive negativity posited, my internal darkness now suddenly become a holistic structure that determines all my moves, my temporal trajectory which for me is pure transience become an itinerary whose past and future are present.

But this object completely escapes me; my subjective existence turns into a being appropriated by a subjectivity irredeemably alien to me. My being is subjected to another, is degraded, abject. My pride is my shame.

My existence is henceforth a striving to hold together my schizoid being, to make the corporeality I am proud of and ashamed of in the fields of others coincide with the corporeality I am for myself—make that object there coincide with the *here* from which I perceive and extend my forces. Whatever happens in the contention with others, it is always my own being that is at stake, and not simply accouterments or the powers and riches of which the exterior world is the reservoir—not an appropriation of any being that is not my own. I am thrown up against others by the inmost demands of my own constitution, by the demand to be. From now on my consciousness aims at being—at a being that is mine and that does exist, but that has been alienated from me.

Encountering the other subjectivity is mortifying. Dealing with his objectivity runs up against the resistance every object offers my powers; but the greatest, the insuperable, difficulty is just in encountering the other as he is, a subjectivity that is one and anyone, everywhere and beyond any where—and is incarnate in the world of objects. All the maneuvers of social concourse are but stratagems to occupy that position where what he truly is can be seen, so that I can come to stand in what I am.

The project is doomed to defeat. I must make contact with alien subjectivity in order to reach my own being, but contact can only be the capture and negation of my freedom—or the objectification, subjugation, of the other. The objectification does not contain his subjectivity and make of it a mundane phenomenon, but obliterates it and my own objectivity with it. All social relations oscillate between phases of respect already enslaving and of conquest already subverted. The confrontation with the other's subjectivity cannot be sustained, because it is the intolerable experience of the alienation of my being, and the apprehensiveness that knows this alienation is already a project to objectify the other. But the other cannot be maintained as an object either, because this object was posited for no other reason than to capture in it the threatening subjectivity of the other, which instead vanishes as the objective form of a body congeals. The defeat of the project I pursue in the face of others will occur many times and in many forms, and each time the defeat functions to formulate the same project again in reversed terms.

4. *The Wiles of Love*

For Sartre human relations are elaborated concretely in an alternation of love and sexual desire. Devotion to the subjectivity of another is love; sexual desire is the concrete form of every project to possess that subjectivity. They are contraries; the one arises from the collapse of the other. Both aim at an integral presence of the other, where one's own integral being could be appropriated. Language[6] and masochism are variants of love; willful indifference and sadism variants of sexual desire; collaboration, conflict, rivalry, emulation, commitment, and obedience are concrete figures of love and sexual desire. Hatred is not the opposite of love, but the will to annihilate both modes of alterity entirely.

Love is the prizing not of the objective traits of the other, corporeal or personal, aesthetic or ethical, but of his or her subjectivity, approaching it and bringing it close to oneself by becoming an object worthy of its total attention. The subjectivity of another is a sovereignty; contact with it means capture and subjugation, one's objectification. Love is the project of making one's subjugation captivating to the captor. Adoration is importunate; love demands to be loved.

The lover takes the initiative, acts, in order to congeal into a pure object. One offers oneself without reserve, gives everything; one is out to draw the full force of the alien subjectivity upon oneself. One lays oneself open, denudes oneself, but with suggestive gestures—acts that, through their inventiveness, their complication, suggest an incalculable tangle of real and potential forces beneath them, a depth of soul. One's moves are not undertakings but uncoverings. By their effectiveness at disrupting discussion, thought, work, by their power to scandalize, they aim to show one's "connections"— the extent to which a whole social and material order of things is objectively bound up with oneself.

The lover seeks to be involved in everything the other does, as the terminus of all his or her movements in the field of things. Everything in the world of objects becomes a means to touch an alien subjectivity. Through one's skills, position, connections, the world is bound up with oneself and offered with oneself. One becomes an object posited in the world, but no longer a relay point toward further objects, no longer used, no longer open to manipulation.

One's devotion to the other, one's giving of oneself over to him or her, in fact aims to put one's own initiatives behind the other's. Love demands that the lover be taken as the object worthy of motivating all the other's moves, demands that the beloved betray trust and friendship, kin and compatriots for the lover. Love is not the element out of which justice or the civic sense is built; it asks for criminality in the subjectivity it adores.

Captivating object, plenitude of significance and being, I shall be the pivot about which the other situates persons, places, and things, the point of insertion of the other's subjectivity into the physical and social world. The subjectivity that I draw upon myself then no longer subjugates me but depends on me. In solitude my subjectivity freely roamed its own world; now I am embedded into objectivity as the pivot about which the other's existence elaborates the objective physical and social world inaccessible to me.

Now the least contingency of my objective form and the contingency of my being at all become unqualifiedly precious and worthy of all the attention of an unrestricted subjectivity. All my existence is justified and it justifies the whole world; such is the transfigured state to which the lover is rapt; such is the joy of love.

The longing to love someone is not an urge that develops on the periphery of a life, a supplementary longing. Conscious life is a craving for being, and love is the absolute form such a self-affirmation can take. Life craves the alien subjectivity

with all its subjective forces and out of the constituent structure of its being.

The quest for what is called wisdom originates, Sartre says,
in this project—the Platonic eros is philosophical. Wisdom is
life motivated by an intuition of the totality; it requires that
one situate oneself not in oneself nor in one's own field of
nutriments and complements but in the whole. A cognitive
project of this sort does not derive from the problem-solving
employment of the mind, the theory that arises out of and is
motivated by praxis. Nor does it derive from the will to put all
things in perspective, intelligence at the service of the will to
sovereignty—the type of intelligence Nietzsche saw in philosophy, the most spiritual form of the will to power. The
project of embedding oneself utterly in universal objective being, and of holding on that being a sovereign gaze with which
one will ecstatically identify oneself, is the very project of
love. The love of wisdom is a love of love.

The compulsion to love cannot but arise in a being like
ourselves, one whose non-being (escaping oneself, being free,
being conscious) is only for the sake of positing itself in being.
And it can only fail.

In the measure that another finds my existence admirable,
valuable, precious, something to be possessed, he or she is
maintained before me in his or her subjectivity, but my existence is subordinated to finalities beyond itself. It can be un-
conditionally affirmed only insofar as the other is captivated
by it. For the other to freely maintain this state is to devote
himself or herself to what maintains my objective form captivating by all its seductive initiatives—my subjectivity. From
being captivated by my objective form he or she shifts to being
fascinated with the subjective force behind that object—comes
to love me. But for me to find myself loved is to find myself
thrown back on to my own responsibility, my own efforts to
be—which but detach themselves from the being they strive to
posit.

Insofar as the seduction succeeds, the other freely subjects
himself or herself to the seducer, abdicating the sovereignty
the seducer needed to usurp. Yet the absolute I wanted to
maneuver into position deceives me by loving me, yielding to
the seduction as a chance to be thanks to me. The intersubjectivity of love is a dual project of subjectivity to posit itself in

objectivity, where each defeats the project of the other by failing to will to maintain itself as a subjectivity for the sake of the other. Love turns in a vicious circle where each seeks in the other an absolute and provokes only an abject longing to love.

In addition, the sovereignty in which one seeks to maintain the other deteriorates in the face of any third party whose glance situates both oneself and one's beloved in the field of relativities which is the world. I find myself demanding sovereign subjectivity from what suddenly turns out to be but a waitress or a corporation executive, an apparatus for transporting dishes and silverware or a machine for programming the reproduction of dishes and silverware. Part of the impulse to possess one's beloved for oneself alone comes from the necessity of isolating oneself with him or her from the degrading presence of any witness.

Love, this strange demand for redemption that can stake everything on one individual, is not due to an illusion one entertains about a witness who would be only a fellow-being. The abjection of this enterprise before the inevitable indiscretion of others is not merely due to the empirical impossibility of sealing oneself up with one's beloved in some retreat away from the public world. The subjectivity I love can contemplate me with an unmeasured and unrestricted attention, equivalent to what the whole multitude of humanity could give. But at the same time the possibility of his or her objectification before my gaze discloses the possibility of inscribing his or her existence in a panorama of objectivity that is not mine only but exists in itself—and thus is exposed to subjectivity in general. My beloved is a sovereignty not only susceptible to being objectified by my initiative, but exposed to anyone; this liability is the shame I feel in demanding love from a being that is of the world.

The shame in all mundane love makes masochism comprehensible. It is an exasperated project of prostration that seeks to forestall any weakness in the other, any tendency to abdicate, by encumbering his or her way with an object that is nothing but an object and which is oneself. But the alien subjectivity masochism contrives to maintain will never be redemptive. This kind of initiative can only make one's existence into something the other can value, utilize, and possess; but the other thereby always subordinates me to extrinsic

ends, always goes beyond me. The more totally I make myself
an object, the less I make myself all objectivity for the other.
The other will use the subjectivity I so totally will in him or
her to subordinate my objectivity to other objects.

If the subjectivity of the other proves forever unequal to the
demands love makes on it, at least one is compensated by
being delivered from the danger an alien subjectivity represented. Subjectivity now turns out to want to be loved by me,
to want my subjectivity. And one begins to see that the absolute subjectivity one demanded, having proved vulnerable,
can be taken possession of. This possibility is that of sexual
appropriation; sexual desire emerges from the deceptions of
love.

Sartre's phenomenological analysis of love discerns in love
an intentional structure rather than a rhythm of intensities,
crests and troughs of impulse. He accounts for the flux and
reflux of exaltation in terms of the logic of the project which
love pursues.

In the exaltation of love one feels one's impulses rising up
before the gaze of a sovereign subjectivity that summons them;
one feels the organic density of one's body galvanized into
deeds which that subjectivity calls for, contracting meaning
and unconditional worth as soon as they emerge into the light
of another's gaze. One's impulses are not obscure disturbances
of a biological or psychic existence ignorant of itself, but
enactments that have sense in themselves, supported by the
whole layout of the objective world that they climax, whose
obscure longings they accomplish. Not only are the pulses of
my life a generous plenitude for which a sovereign subjectivity exists, but my justified existence justifies the objective universe in which it exists.

Yet this *sense* that one's existence acquires suddenly in the
ecstasy of love is as thin and evanescent as the functional
significance attached to the root of the chestnut tree and the
social utility attached to the park bench proves to be before the
specter of brute being in *Nausea*. The vertigo Roquentin feels
in the park turns with an intimation of the ultimate non-
coincidence of sense with presence, the contingency of all the
coordinates, system, order, functionality imposed on being,

which suddenly vacillate like the shimmer of nothingness which all these determinations—which are negations—in fact are. In *Being and Nothingness* nausea figures as the distinctive feeling one has for one's own being—a feeling of insipidity and weight, of the drag of being behind the thrusts of the projects that give it sense. One can feel completely swept away into the sense and worth one has for another, but the other's subjectivity proves to be a vortex not intense enough to ensure this ecstasy. Existence is not as good as its ecstasy, and in the feeling of weight and staleness at the core of the massive and dumb organism one feels again the evanescence of sense and the pointless obstinacy of being.[7]

5. *The Sexual Intention*

Sartre seats the sexual impulse in subjectivity itself. Libido is not a force or energy-thrust emerging into consciousness; it is an integral way one's entire subjectivity can be structured. Sexual desire is not to be derived from physical processes in the chemical secretions and nervous charges of the genital organs, nor from a physiological stratum of circuits that would be observable from without and intelligible in objective terms. Consciousness is not the zone where the libido is disguised or transfigured; rather, consciousness is through and through libidinous, the libido is a certain form of subjectivity. The philosophical and reflexive analysis of the structure of consciousness will disclose the nature of the sexual impulse. The sexual instinct will no longer be viewed from the outside, where it can appear as an anonymous generic force in the individual, destining the psychic forces and feelings of the individual to the service of the species. As a structure of consciousness it is a form of existence that exists *for itself.*

Sexuality derives directly from the objectifying impact on consciousness of an alien consciousness; it is one of the fundamental ways of assimilating that impact. It is this intent—and not biological finality—that makes one's given being, one's body, a sex organ.

The sexual impulse is entirely addressed to the other; it is intentional. It is the second fundamental mode of relating to the other. Sexual sensibility is not a susceptibility to sensuous stimuli or sense data; it relates with the other as a whole. It deals with the other in his or her essential existence and essential alterity, a force structuring the world into his or her own situation, a force that is essentially alien and alienating.

The Sexual Object

How will intentional analysis make sexual desire intelligible? As it does for every subjective structure—by its term, its object. This object is transcendent, exterior; it is alterity itself, the other. What sexual desire desires is not any kind of immanent phenomenon; the pleasure or tension-relaxation that one may feel reflexively are but a second, concomitant object of libidinous consciousness. They are the sense of the taut or languid tonus of a craving that is made determinate by an exterior objective.

Nor is the sexual impulse the feeling of a force building up to a determinate action, copulation. There are two arguments: sexual desire exists in young children, who have not yet learned to perform the act of copulation, and in the aged and the castrated, who are no longer able to perform it. Secondly, copulation in fact terminates sexual desire. But sexual desire does not desire to terminate itself; it is itself voluptuous, it wishes to intensify and prolong itself, to be.

One sexually desires somebody—some body; sexual desire is neither attraction for a mind nor fascination with a personality. It is mortal flesh and blood we crave, and not, as Plato's Socrates taught, the splendor of eternity, eternal beauty. It is his or her objectivity, corporeality, that situates the other before one and before one's desire—not a specific trait of that corporeality different from one's own, not primary or secondary gender characteristics which one's own body would lack. Sexual desire is not essentially heterosexual. But it is not so much matter and tissue and blood that one desires, but the body as a whole. And a body that is alive, that is, a body that relates to its surroundings, a body "in situation," given as an incarnate subjectivity. The carnal is objectified subjectivity, where the objectification does not obliterate the subjectivity but contains it.

The Subjective Form of the Sexual Intention

Such an intuition has a distinctive subjective form. Sexual desire is not a clear and transparent envisaging of something outside itself, like the hunger for a certain food or the wish for a certain implement. The craving for another's body affects one with a feeling of one's own skin and muscles and one's own breathing. It is a movement weighted down with its own site in being, a craving for another which adheres to its own longing, feels its own drag, in languor. It does not flee one's own body, like a glance which darts from the eyes toward its objective. Not that sexual desire would have to view its object through the opaqueness of one's own body—one desires out of one's being, with one's body. The erection of the penis, tumescence of the nipples, moist and trembling hands, rise in body temperature, are not blind substance interfering with a consciousness that seeks to open upon the outside; it is to them that the sexual object is addressed. Unlike the sense one can have of one's hunger, which can consider it with a detached reflective consideration, or keep it out of the focus of consciousness by turning to other things, the sense of themselves that sexual impulses produce become accomplices of these impulses, become themselves lustful. Sexual desire is prostrate with regard to itself, affected with its own being, a swooning rather than a stance. And it assents to the weight of its being for itself, desires its own contingency.

The Telos of the Libido

In this turgid desire Sartre uncovers a project of appropriation. Lust schemes at getting close to the other in the flesh, an incarnate subjectivity, to make him or her one's own, make him or her exist for-oneself.

The objectified other was first encountered in action, a posture poised before instruments, a self-moving, working configuration in a field of gear, who could therefore be useful for one's own ends. Sexual desire wishes to undo this hold the other has on the world, and the hold one had on him or her in objectifying him or her. Its unpragmatic praxis aims to make the other one's own by disconnecting the finalities in which his or her objective being puts him or her; its telos is the other's presence no longer teleological. Disconnected from his or her gear, the other is there without intermediaries in the intimacy of the sexual hold. And as the sexual desire effects this incarnation of another, it sinks into its own weight of being, is possessed by its own carnality.

The movements of sexual desire are caresses. The hand, which is not only an apparatus for grasping and taking, an instrument for discovering and feeling, a sense organ, and a contrivance for gesturing, an expressive organ, is also an organ for caressing, a sex organ. The eyes are not only organs for penetrating, exposing, or discovering, sense organs, and organs for approaching, having, and inhabiting, organs of appropriation. For there are also looks that caress. Even the least dexterous and blindest parts of the body—belly, thighs, breasts, buttocks—are organs for caressing; they are indeed especially so.

The other to whom the caresses are addressed was a posture, a series of gestures and operations. One sees musculature tensing and taut, frame held erect, in position for its tasks, or disequilibrating itself for locomotion, one sees hands pushing and grasping. Its clothing is protection against the dirt, abrasions, and weather its action exposes it to, and is always to some extent a uniform, situating the wearer in a social context—is always to some extent apparel that "suits one," that defines and displays an identity. The caress moves to disconnect this mundane presence. It reduces the body caressed to a passive relationship with the gear and implements about it, strips it of its clothing, its functioning, significance, and identity. The caresses that wander across the body of the other are not exploring but exposing, not gathering tactile impressions but spreading a static of amorphous sensations between the body caressed and its field of operations, so that it no longer captures the signals coming from the outside. This does not mean that there is a reflective consciousness deliberating first and then lining up its own organs and limbs according to its schemes; the purposiveness of this consciousness is not self-reflective and takes form by forming gestures. The lustful hand bears itself toward the hand holding on to the railing of a boat, a contact that invites to indolence, covering it with an unsought-for pleasure, containing a temptation to let go. The caresses undo the functions and the forms of the agent body, shaping the other into sheer carnality. They invite the alien consciousness to return from the far-off objectives of its foreseeing and ordering and adhere to the felt pressure of the caresses under the surface of the body they fondle. They aim to capture and hold that consciousness in the body one embraces and possesses.

Sexual desire is a total modality of life; there is a libidinal form of relationship with the world induced with sexual desire for the other. One lets go of one's own initiatives and sinks into a passive receptivity with regard to the field in which one finds oneself. Things continue to turn their surfaces to one, but now one does not look at them circumspectively, attending to their functions and uses. One addresses only their material opacity, their gritty, smooth, tepid, greasy, or rough substance as it comes in contact with one's own flesh; one fondles the warmth, the humidity, the sunlight that bathes one, the grass that tickles and whose green paste fills one's eyes, the candlelight that illuminates the implements on the table less than it illuminates itself, glows. One caresses things and lets oneself be caressed by them; one feels the rudeness of objects, the cacophony of their concourse as painful caresses, things fondling one with anticaresses.

To desire sexually is already to begin to get close to someone and to things and to begin to fondle them. The sexual impulse is consciousness in the fondling and caressing look, and if it is implicitly conscious of itself, this awareness is itself lustful. The fondling hand becomes turgid and passive, it no longer grasps or pulls or manipulates but rubs spasmodically against things, dragging itself in place; the desire in it is weighted down with itself. The fingers are no longer antennae that can tighten up over an obstacle and manipulate it whatever its shape; they fall limp and inert on the end of the hand that caresses. The lover ceases to have a posture mobilized for tasks and obstacles and becomes a trembling mass of substance bearing itself over to another flesh. Possessed by an enterprise of appropriation and laden with himself or herself, the lover is held within the mass of his or her own substance.

The Motivation for Lust

In Sartre's existential analysis this carnal craving appears as an option, revealing the essential freedom of consciousness.

Conscious life itself determines itself to contract this form of intentional behavior. When a hand begins to creep over to the hand of another that holds on to the railing, to fondle it, we shall not be able to locate a cause of that movement in an exterior stimulus or in an antecedent local event in the organism; this movement of the hand is part of a structuring that the whole conscious system is contracting, of itself. This body is relaxing its axis, becoming languid, giving itself a new internal rhythm, a heavy respiration, a pulse that begins to pound, a tonus that grows turgid—it is ceasing to be mobilized by a practical intention, its consciousness is sinking into its own dense being. The conscious desire for the presence of the other as flesh, and no longer as supporter, collaborator or interlocutor, is arising, is taking form in all that. In this autodetermination Sartre recognizes an option and the freedom of consciousness.

The sexual impulse is from the first intentional, desire for the other, presence in view of a future. And like every structure that forms in the stream of a life this present relates back to the prior phase. It is not really caused by that past phase, where another structure was in effect, but it measures the distance it is taking from the phase it passes and makes past, gives it the sense of a point of departure from which the present took off, the being from which it came to be—its motive.

The caress which passes lightly over the surfaces of the other, barely grazing the down or touching only the atmosphere above that down, is in fact sounding the depths—divining the alien subjectivity that had receded into those surfaces. It is not only feeling the pleasure of touching the warm, the smooth in flesh, but is seeking to feel the spasms of feeling of the other in his or palpable flesh, is making buttocks, feet, shoulders, back—surfaces turned away from the direction of the other's gaze and perceptions—into organs quivering with receptivity. It moves to provoke motility in the body it touches, motility in regions not touched by the outside things. It wants to free the other from the functions he or she has taken on from the determinate layout of things, the roles he or she has assumed in the social order, the identity he or she has contracted. It wants to feel in the spasms that it induces to disturb the functional forms of that body the freedom of an alien agent; it is trying to touch the judging impulse of the other, feeling its own power to elicit affirmation, the yes yes yes of pleasure in the other. It wants a power capable of obeying as well as violating order in that body; it wants the curses and the blessings by which subjectivity arises, god-conjuring and god-obliterating. In the body it holds, the libidinal consciousness wants the very subjectivity of the other with all its transcending powers; it wants that subjectivity captive, possessed, no longer expropriating.

The movements of lust are incantations rather than techniques. Disconnecting the other has to be done by conjuration; the field of implements has to be not controlled but effaced. One seeks to induce in the other a fascination with one's own nakedness, a fascination that blurs out his or her practical intentionalities. It is not the dexterity of the hands that is most captivating but a hand trailing over the other with trembling and indecisive movements. Indeed the caresses pass from hands to breasts, buttocks, thighs, stomach: flesh saturated with feeling pressing together. A sex organ is not a tool; it is essential that penis and clitoris in erection, the vagina lubricating, not be activated voluntarily, used by a reflective consciousness. No fine, prehensile organ assembled with striated muscles can be a sex organ, Sartre says; a sex organ can only be part of the vegetative system.

The carnalization which one's sexual intention realizes in oneself is, for Sartre, not a common drifting toward a state of presence where neither existence can be a threat any longer for the other because one no longer knows if it is my flesh or his or her own that the other feels ensnared in, no longer knows whose is the feeling adrift in flesh. For Sartre the carnalization is entirely appropriative: I am becoming a body arousing the subjectivity of another, a contingency that is the source of his or her freedom, a brute substance that sparks the upsurgence of alien spontaneity. Yet this carnalization of my own subjectivity is also my own deep aim for myself, not simply a means to ensnare the sovereignty of another. If my subjectivity can be in every case only an enterprise of synthesis, an effort to stabilize the alternating contradiction of subjectivity and objectivity with which the other breaks into my world, to possess an integral experience of myself, it is also an effort to reappropriate into my own consciousness that exteriority, that object-existence which the apparition of the other revealed me to have. It longs to feel for itself too the flesh it exposes to the feeling of another.

The Orgasmic Failure

Yet at the very moment when Sartre's phenomenology exhibits one's own wholeness in the sexual passion, and the wholeness of the other under kisses and caresses, his analysis immediately proceeds—and can only proceed—to demonstrate the failure inherent in this project. The course of sexual impulses themselves produces the disintegration of this wholeness—with the ineluctability with which the kisses and caresses at a certain moment make orgasm inevitable.

The nausea of contingency undermines the passion with which one throws oneself into this enterprise; a desperate and bad faith is involved in one's commitment to it, and explains the vehemence of the commitment. The fusion of consciousness with body, sense with presence, the feeling of being everywhere alive in one's substance, the feeling that every pulse and every mole of one's flesh are significant and gracious, is but an appearance whose seductive and evanescent nothingness explains the purely repetitive character of sexual desire, which can never build on itself. In the underlying taste of nausea clinging to life, nausea which the erotic paroxysm does not conjure, he finds confirmed the deepest convictions of his epistemology and ontology. For him conscious activity is a sort of null-activity, not transitive, not effective, an activity that leaves intact what it illuminates and articulates, adds nothing to what it knows, or adds only the nothingness of contrasts and relationships, and thus truly knows, knows *being as it is*. And consciousness knows too that this is so, that it can experience the evanescence of all the significance it contributes to the brute distribution of being, can catch sight of the absolute contingency and facticity of the root of the chestnut tree and the seat in the bus beneath the names with which nature is articulated and cultural objects constituted. The erotic significance which seemed to bring blind glandular masses out of their stupor and make them exist for themselves seemed to do nothing to them but bring them out in their very being. But this transfiguration is itself nothingness, a shimmering of nothingness that does not conjure what feeling, contact of self with self, the nausea affected with the weight of contingency, knows.

Similarly, the incarnation of the other, that synthetic whole of subjectivity and objectivity which is flesh, can only be a stroboscopic illusion. Appropriation can only be abolition of the other; the hands of lust are those of an assassin. For alterity can appear only as an absence, as the perceived reference of the body that is objectified, comprehendible and graspable, to a subjectivity that would reverse and undermine all my objectification. And that subjectivity itself, which as soon as it appears is everywhere on me, penetrating me to the core of my being, can remain nonetheless apart, other, only by a reference to the imminent possibility of withdrawing totally, leaving everywhere only objects and gear. The impression of flesh, of a subjectivity incarnate, turns out to be nothing more than the perception of a certain type of gesture. It is produced by the perfidious erotic fondling, by disarming and disrobing the other, disconnecting his or her movements from their practical coordinates, reducing them to organic restlessness or spasms of indolence. In the extraterritoriality of the bedroom and before the muteness of lust, the expressivity of the other loses its meaningfulness and is reduced to nonsense, to animal sighs, sobs of pleasure, laughter that hurts, affirmation that negates and negation that affirms. In reality one has not come closer to grasping the subjectivity of another in this dissolute organism that no longer supports its mundane functions or one's own, is gratuitous or superfluous in the world. Lust that thinks it is on the verge of appropriating a transcendent source of meaning and worth is only coming close to the taste of one's own existence which the other, in existing, ever flees—the nausea over pure flesh.

Although Sartre sets out to demonstrate that sexual desire, like every vector of life, is a futile passion, haunted by an ideal of existence in itself and for itself which it itself undermines, his phenomenological explications do not in fact show this failure. His analysis of the experience of another and of oneself in the kisses and caresses nowhere demonstrates anything illusory about the incarnation realized. What his exposition shows is not that the sexual project fails of its own essence, but that it does not *endure*, and that the reasons for the turn into the self-defeating project of sadism lie in the structure of every sexual undertaking. He establishes this by showing that the total caress, the total embrace issues in orgasm, which is not the goal and fulfillment of sexual desire but its collapse.

Sartre does not make the essence of orgasm a topic for eidetic analysis, and his phenomenology includes neither a phenomenological analysis of taking and penetrating, nor a real exposition of pleasure. There are no doubt reasons for this.

What Sartre calls the pure reflection which a consciousness can engage in reveals consciousness as a stream of free and sovereign spontaneity. "Its knowledge is a totality; it is a lightning intuition without relief, without point of departure and without point of arrival. Everything is given at once in a sort of absolute proximity. . . . At the same time it is never surprised by itself; it does not teach us anything but only posits."[8] The consciousness that reflects will experience its pleasure immediately as the "contexture" of its own act, with a qualitative index that differentiates it from other kinds of feeling. Yet if pleasure is a pure trembling of the subjective spontaneity, what could be a pleasure felt in one's being, one's facticity, in the incarnation in one's body? Would we not, like Kant, have to distinguish between the affectivity that affects the spontaneity of our consciousness, and that which affects our receptivity? Is not voluptuousness something like a craving—for *what* one knows not—that is pleasurable, and that is continually perplexed by itself and surprises itself?

The sense of one's own body given in Sartre's pure reflection is always that of a viewpoint from which the view opens, a point of departure, a being quit; it is conceptualized as one's own being, posited in reality, but always transcended or surpassed, past. For this reason a real sense of action is lacking in Sartre's phenomenology; intentionality is not the inner diagram of a body's own movements, it is an insubstantial movement proceeding out of the body. If the body's moves appear intentional, they so appear in the eyes of a witness who perceives them comprehensively in view of their mundane correlates. But as successive phases of a body lodged in being, *movements* have to be described as a pure multiplicity of "upsurgences" and "abolitions" in being; the "abrupt appearance of synthetic unity in space" is in fact, Sartre has said, "a counterfeit which collapses immediately into the infinite multiplicity of exteriority."[9] Thus there is not an intentionality seen bearing a body; there is rather an intentional way of synthesizing brute occurrences of being which one witnesses.[10]

The ontological poverty of Sartre's concept of movement and the insubstantiality of his concept of pleasure is reflected in the thin character of his phenomenological exegesis of orgasm. One's body become orgasmic becomes grasping, manipulating, penetrating—a succession of disincarnate operations on a mass of limbs and orifices. The contact produces more intense surface pleasure, but these rivet attention to oneself—and one forgets the goal of all these frenzied manipulations. Sartre has not in fact circumscribed orgasm itself; he has but decomposed it into pleasure and penetration, which are not seen to have properly erotic meaning. Voluptuous pleasure has been assimilated to pleasure in general, and orgasmic movements to pragmatic operations.

The movement of sexual desire was from the start appropriative, a project of getting close to another, making him or her exist for oneself. This appropriation is not realized simply where one sees oneself making subjectivity exist in an object one holds, provoking the ripples of pleasure and torment that agitate it. The libidinous consciousness wishes to reach the other without quitting itself. It takes the form of a body that seeks to penetrate the body of another and absorb it into itself through all its orifices.

Sartre's ontology of being and nothingness is surely contrived to comprehend the existence of *orifices in being* and the compulsion of consciousness to fill them with itself. The attraction for holes exists as a tendency to put one's finger, one's arm into the hole; a hole is an appeal to one's being. It exists as a negative or empty form of oneself—and thus suggests that one is oneself a fullness. The ideal hole would be an excavation that I can squeeze into completely, thereby bringing about fullness of being with what I am.[11] The project of conscious existence—which of itself is pure aiming, nonbeing—is always to sacrifice oneself in order that the totality, plenitude of being, exist; the preoccupation with holes is a specific mundane form of it. Attention to holes is then not to be derived from physiological lacks, hungers, or from the pleasures of infantile anal sexuality. The infant's discovery of the contours of his own body is secondary and derivative; his tendency to fill up his own orifices, and the contentment this yields, is an instance of the general tendency to fill orifices in objectivity with one's own substance. The preoccupation with lacks and wants and with the penetrating and filling of them has to be understood out of the nature of consciousness—its being as a longing to be—and is not made comprehensible by saying that consciousness is produced by sublimation of anal-oral compulsions. "When [an infant] puts his fingers in his mouth, he tries to wall up the holes in his face; he expects that his finger will merge with his lips and the roof of his mouth and block up the buccal orifice as one fills the crack in a wall with cement; he seeks again the density, the uniform and spherical plenitude of Parmenidean being; if he sucks his thumb, it is precisely in order to dissolve it, to transform it into a sticky paste which will seal the hole of his mouth."[12] The first form of eating is eating oneself, filling a hole one has discovered with one's own limb or member, sacrificing one's life in order that being in itself be full; the substance of the world can become nutriment because it has already been identified with one's own substance and can substitute for one's own flesh to fill one's mouth. Appetite is not a will to devour the world in order that one's life alone subsist; it is the compulsion to fill oneself up in order that the plenum of objective being alone be. One does not go to restaurants for restauration; one eats in order to fill oneself.

Were we to pick up and carry further Sartre's line of exposition, one would say that the compulsion to penetrate a mouth, anus, navel, vagina, and to stuff penis, breasts, fingers, nose, tongue, in one's mouths are cases of the general tendency to penetrate and fill; they acquire their sexual significance from the part they play in the sexual project, the project of appropriating an incarnate subjectivity. They are sexually effectual inasmuch as by using one's own incarnated subjectivity, all one's feeling compacted in the tumescent penis, in the formless and functionless tongue, to fill the hole in another, one fills the body that is there with spasms of savage and dense feeling, the yes yes yes to pleasure. One's own flesh in this orifice is what was lacking to make the disconnected and nonfunctioning body of another into flesh saturated with subjectivity. And even as one filled one's own

orifices with one's own flesh, sacrificing one's projective life
in order that a plenum of being be, one fills one's orifices with
the tongue, penis, fingers, buttocks of another, using the flesh
of another to realize one's own incarnation. That the vagina is
a mouth, its false lips castrating, does not mean that the genital
movements are to be understood by reducing them to more
general kinds of movement, those of eating and assimilating,
or destroying. The dismembering that the castrating vagina
aims at is that of the functional or pragmatic body; it is simultaneously production of a plenitude to appear in an orifice.
Such would be orgasm envisaged as a behavior dealing with
orifices—rather than as manipulations, as praxis.

Yet, pursuing his will to prove that the sexual project defeats itself, Sartre forgets the possible analysis of the eidos
orgasm, and does assimilate its movements to techniques. The
orgasmic body, he says, is seizing, pulling, biting, twisting; to
become orgasmic is to cease to be flesh and to become an
instrument handling an implement in the midst of a pragmatic
field. The sense of feeling and wild affirmation playing on the
surfaces of the other dissipates; all one has in one's hands is an
organic mass assimilating gasses, circulating its fluids, exud-
ing its secretions. The more efficient one becomes the more
completely does the flesh which one set out to appropriate
vanish; one is like a sleepwalker who wakens to find himself
gripping the bedstead and no longer able to recall the night-
mare that provoked this reaction.[13]

Sadism follows. It is a project of realizing the incarnation
of alien subjectivity by force and no longer by incantation and
contagion. The sadist wants the incarnation of the other but
wills efficacious coldness in himself or herself. For the sadist
has come upon a power that affects the subjectivity of another
instrumentally—the power to produce pain. Pain is entirely
subjective; it is the tonus of subjectivity affecting itself. The
suffering of pain is subjectivity wrenching away from itself, its
very wrenchings afflicted with themselves, themselves painful. A sadist uses pain to make the consciousness of another be
mired in itself, unendurable to itself, held in itself from flight
to the exterior. The prostrate subjectivity of pain disfigures a
body, producing obscenity. Its struggles only manifest its impotence and contingency.

The sadist wants freedom in the victim's body, wants the other wilfully to assent to his or her abjection and to crave impotence as the most intense sensation of existing. Here sadism is very close to love. Love seeks an abject usage of the other's freedom by means of a monumentalization of the lover's objective being. Sadism seeks abasement of the other through a technology of corporeal prowess. The failure of sadism reverts to, reverses into, love.

For sadism also produces its own failure. When the moment of assent occurs, when the victim wills his or her pain and obscenity, the victim's body no longer maintains itself as an organized instrumentality of functions tempting the sadist's capabilities, and closes in on itself. It becomes a panting, sweating mass of organs producing pain in itself by all its convulsions, an obscene and absurd mass that cannot be of any use of the sadist. The terminal absurdity of the sadistic project explains its tenaciousness; the torturer continues to torture because he or she has nothing else to do with the victim.

However able one may be to elicit betrayal and self-abasement from one's victim, there always subsists the irreducible difference between the subjectivity one sees tangible in flesh and the power that sees one, the difference constitutive of the alterity of the other. The subjectivity that the sadist has in his or her grasp is but the indeterminism of spasmodic movements producing sensations in a body, after-images of internal stimuli. How far that is from the subjectivity he or she aimed to appropriate becomes abruptly evident when the bloodshot membranes of the eyes of the victim no longer occlude his look. Even at the last moment of abjection, before all life expires out of the organism tortured—even after that expiration—that look comes, to objectify and to judge the barren and desperate exertions of the sadist over some obscene organism.

Is orgasm itself sadism? Sartre has assimilated the orgasmic convulsions, the movements of penetration and being penetrated by tumescent gland unable to control itself, with manipulations. That is why for him all the force involved in orgasm only serves to awaken, out of its spellbound lust, an

agent consciousness, imminently sadistic. The agitations of
the orgasmic body produce heightened surface pleasure, but
the very pleasure of orgasmic voluptuousness motivates attention to one's pleasure and to oneself, and thus also awakens
consciousness from its lust.

Sartre has not attempted to delineate what is distinctive
about voluptuous pleasure as pleasure. He has specified it by
its object—by the sense or significance of its object: a body
sensuously perceived as manifesting agitations of sensibility,
of feeling. But he has not specified what makes up the sensual
quality of this pleasure. Yet this would be required by his
"psychoanalysis of things," which must explicate their
specific ways of being *this*, their qualitative opaqueness, and
the specific sensuous modes of their apprehension. It is one of
the vaunted superiorities of phenomenological ontology that it
requires, and makes possible, such an analysis. Pleasure is a
sensible consciousness that apprehends a qualitative presence—in this case, that of flesh; it is not just a matter of contingent and blind "tastes." Existential psychoanalysis must yield
an essential understanding of the quality felt and the feeling.

Yet Sartre consigns sexual pleasure, as a pure contingency,
to the unfounded and the unintelligible, even going so far as to
assert that it is a pure contingency that it exists at all. Like any
feeling, voluptuous pleasure is a mode of lateral self-
consciousness, a way consciousness is conscious not of its
signifying intention but of its being, its body, its contingency.
He explains that in orgasmic struggles the intensifying pleasure finally provokes attention to itself. To the extent that
one's own body and pleasure become the object of reflective
attention the incarnate presence of the other sinks into the
background and sexual desire loses sight of its objective. To
the extent that the other turns into a means to realize one's
own objectification in one's own eyes, that the pleasure of
caressing becomes a pleasure of being caressed, one's consciousness fills with a sense of the stale contingency of one's
own body, a nausea. The moment of masochism is at hand.

The inevitability of the collapse of sexual desire into
masochism derives from the Sartrean principle that reflection
poisons feeling. Feeling is the lateral awareness of an intention's own reality; inasmuch as the awareness returns from its

external object to objectify its own being, the contexture of that consciousness inevitably changes. Reflection objectifies, puts at a distance, and is self-nihilating. It is cold.

Might not pleasure's incessant movement of self-affirmation have an affective and not objectifying form—self-affirmation as adhesion to self, itself pleasurable—a lust lustful with regard to itself? No doubt objectifying reflection on one's melancholy already limits and dissipates it. But there are also involutions of feeling, a sense of one's melancholy that is itself melancholy, a sadness sad over its sadness, deepening in spirals. The thesis that pleasure is itself the failure and not the fulfillment of sexual desire, that it inevitably produces its own collapse, depends on the thesis that every consciousness and every self-consciousness tends to the objectifying form. And this in turn expresses Sartre's central conviction that consciousness desires to give itself the mode of being of objects—to posit itself in a being that would be permanent presence to the point of self-identity, solid, massive, intransient.

6. *The Bad Faith of Sex*

Sartre has identified being in itself affirmed—absolutely there in itself and through and through significant, ground of itself, being-in-itself-for-itself—to be the telos of amorous and of sexual striving, and indeed of every intention. This telos has the structure of God, is value itself, and all value-phenomena are figures of this ideal. Every human existence is a passion in that its project is to lose itself so as to *found* being, to set forth being as a coherent manifestation. The world for us came into being out of the vain effort to create God.

The other, inasmuch as he or she is a subjectivity posited in the world, a being that exists in itself but also for itself, is from the first a figure of value. The alterity of the other appears in the reference of a subjectivity to an objectivity and of an objectivity to a subjectivity; but this reference is, we have seen, the absence of the one from the other. This figure of value is absence itself—sacred. But alterity becomes present in the appropriation effected in sexual intimacy. The passion of sexual passion is the project of giving oneself, losing oneself, in order that there be the absolute intimacy with a subjectivity completely objectified and an objectivity conscious throughout—concrete existential figure of value, of God.

This value makes our existence significant or eloquent. We have seen that love speaks; it is my objective being wholly addressed to the other. Indeed, language itself is originally not communication of information but a means of seduction.[14] The lover aims to make his or her objective presence absolutely significant, such that all the sense of the world will derive from it. But sexual caresses aim to disconnect the world and silence its unending referentiality. They therefore do not, like the gestures of the expressive body, mean something. The caressing body does not give only signs to another, but gives itself. It has another eloquence.

Every desire for being—every modality of consciousness inasmuch as it is intentional, a consciousness *of* something—is a desire to be. It nihilates itself, evacuates its space, in order to maintain itself as a desire for a being. It wants that being not only to be there but to be desired still. The ideal of hunger is the food present but the hunger present too, appetite coextensive with food. The disappointment that comes with repletion refers not to the inadequacy of the being that was assimilated, which would have proved unequal to the hunger that desired it, but rather to the inadequacy of the desire, which is escaping itself. For the desire desires to have the kind of being possessed by what it desires; it wishes to *be*, with the solidity, faultless identity, fixity, of being in itself. It aims at a substantial, statuesque version of itself. A consciousness that desires suffers, but suffering tends not to anesthetize itself but to feel itself; it suffers from not suffering enough, it aims to mold a noble or true figure of itself.[15] "If I must suffer, I should prefer that my suffering would seize me and flow over me like a storm. . . . Each groan, each facial expression of the man who suffers aims at sculpturing a statue-in-itself of suffering."[16] If man is "the being that is in question in his being," this questioning does not strive to resolve itself, but to become a rhetorical question, speech that does not call for a reply, or that is its own reply and fulfillment.

Such also are the torments of lust. The sexual caresses congeal as they sensitize the substance of the other. Sexual desire does not take form in the absence of its object, to be extinguished when its object is there. What it desires is there from the start; it is a desire provoked by the presence of the desirable, and it only seeks to become desire utterly. It aims to project itself into the identity and weight of being in itself or into the completeness and plenitude that an artwork has; sensuality aims to realize a noble or aesthetic ideal of itself. This ideal identity of lust with rhetoric, of the orgasmic with the statuesque, is the poetry of sex. In lust, life suffers and torments itself not in order to obtain release of its longing, satiation, and return to the inertia of the inorganic, but in order to attain the higher inertia of the poetic.

Yet Sartre is determined to make the phenomenological analysis of the sexual relationship show that the spirit cannot be incarnated, that its debauched belief that it has been is in bad faith, that its poetics is but rhetoric. The other, a concrete figure of value, a presence everywhere significant, a contingency wholly desired, is so only as absence—as the reference of his subjective force to a possible objective evidence and the reference of his objective form to the subjectivity it hides. And the statuesque figure of itself which lust strains to maintain can only be the trace of the passing of a desire that is want of being through and through. In fact, sexual desire takes itself too seriously; the *esprit de serieux*—believing that what it values *is* and consigns to human existence a mission and a destiny—is always in bad faith.

7. The Value of Freedom

Sartre demonstrates that sexual desire is an enterprise that projects its own failure and believes in itself only with bad faith, and he repeats the same demonstration with love, sadism and masochism, indifference and language, and hatred. *Being and Nothingness* is throughout a diagnosis of the bad faith of the passion of an existence that, in all its serious undertakings, sacrifices itself in the effort to realize God. This treatise could only have been written in the perspective of a possible authenticity, of which there is very brief, but decisive, mention. Sartre's book must itself be a work of pure reflection.

The conversion to authenticity requires that consciousness return, with the lucidity of a pure reflection, upon its existence, and will to be for itself the flight from itself which constitutes it as something that exists for itself. The project can be stated only in contradictory terms, for authentic existence also encloses its contradiction within itself. It will have to bind itself to its own freedom. It will have to affirm, to posit, its utter negativity. It will have to return reflectively upon itself in a movement that removes it ever more manifestly from itself. It will have to appropriate its existence as self-expropriation. It will have to desire to be continual lack of being.

It would seem that the immediate form of the conversion to authenticity—"when freedom will become conscious of itself and will reveal itself in anguish as the unique source of value and the nothingness by which the *world* exists"[17]—will be nihilistic. For can one want values when one knows that nothing is behind them, that nothingness is behind them? And can "freedom take itself for a value inasmuch as it is the source of all value"[18] once it sees that that source—utterly insubstantial, purely relative, relating operation—is a desire for the impossible absolute being? Sartre had declared the Heideggerian authenticity, which consists in a freedom to die, impossible; if life's projection of itself unto its death is experienced as anxiety, that is because life can only will life, existence can only will being. But if existence now recognizes that it is a pure expenditure of itself in the vain effort to create absolute being, God, what could be the worth of such a source of value for it?

The conversion to authenticity, the upsurgence of a purifying reflection, can only appear unmotivated and gratuitous in a life that hitherto consisted in desiring to posit itself in being. Value is now seen to be posited by freedom; it becomes possible alongside other possibilities. The devaluing of value makes the world appear in its irreducible contingency and in the unfoundedness, or foundational absurdity, of its being. Life loses its seriousness and becomes ludic. The reign of the sacred and the magical gives way to play, sole value or gratuity of the postmetaphysical age. The waiter in the café who plays at being a waiter will henceforth only play at playing waiter.

The games we play today are not pure expenditure; they are forms of the desire to be and to have. Through the rules, forms, and skills with which freedom binds itself, the ludic activity aims to fix itself in being, desire aims at the statu-esque. The player strives to become an athlete, in the sense that the waiter strives to be a waiter. And these activities are projects of appropriation: skiing, mountain climbing, swim-ming are, Sartre showed, enterprises of conquering and pos-sessing the indomitable and unutilizable elements, more seri-ous still than work for wages.[19]

What then might a sexual desire be that has lost all its seriousness, that has ceased to be seduction, incantation, magic, and has become sheer play? Is it not perhaps essential to sexuality that it does not know what it wants or what it is doing? Yet Sartre has defined sexual desire by a subjective teleology. Its moves are sexual, caresses, inasmuch as they intend to divest the other of his or her apparatus and apparel and hold a disarmed and denuded sovereignty contained in the nonfunctional materiality of his or her flesh. How could a subjectivity that comes to will itself explicitly and uncondi-tionally to be free not commit itself to subjugate every alien sovereignty? On the other hand, sexual desire is realized in caresses, as thought in language; the desire which caresses assents to its own incarnation. This sensual relapse of one's subjectivity into one's own body is lived as one's presence in all its contingency become everywhere significant and everywhere responsive. Sartre has shown its voluptuousness to be made of an ecstatic idealization of one's existence, one's reality becoming a value for the other and in oneself.

What then could be the sexual form of desire that "chooses not to recover itself but to flee itself, not to coincide with itself but to be always at a distance from itself"?[20] What could be a desire for the other that is no longer appropriative but expro-priative, a desire that no longer experiences the alien subjectiv-ity as a sovereignty to be vanquished? With what hand will such a desire touch the other, with what gratuitous touch of playful hands that no longer seek to mold a statue of living flesh, hands that have lost all their poetry?

With Sartre, phenomenological analysis applied to sexual life reveals a metaphysical drama. The love and the sexuality Sartre has examined are projects to appropriate an objective being; they are passions in which the insubstantiality of conscious existence sacrifices itself in order to realize value. The analysis is thus at the same time a critique of bad faith, and invokes the possibility of authenticity—where insubstantial conscious existence in the midst of being produces sense, and wills to exist for this insubstantial and gratuitous production. But Sartre's account of the objectives, subjective form, and motivations of love and sexuality show bad faith and inauthenticity in their constitution. To imagine a sexuality that is not formed for the sake of an ideal of being but that engenders and answers to sense would require a different concept of sense than that which is fundamental to Sartre—for whom sense is relationship, contrast, differentiation, that is, negation, shimmering of nothingness over the surfaces of a being which, beneath, remains stolidly what it is in itself. For Maurice Merleau-Ponty, phenomenology makes possible a new conception of sense. In explicating it, he will show that the possible sexuality that engenders and answers to sense is our sexuality.

2.

Sense and Non-sense in Sexuality

Sartre had seen an affective force behind the objectification of our bodies; Maurice Merleau-Ponty used phenomenology to explore the metaphysical preconceptions behind the privilege that empiricist physiology and psychology had bestowed on the objective image of the body. And to reveal another body—the "lived body."

Like Sartre, Merleau-Ponty distinguishes between our body as object and our body as agent. But for him the distinction is not between the way my body appears to others and the way it appears to me. For Sartre my own body is for me but an unperceived, unmanipulated, and unfelt locus about which the spectacle of attracting and repelling implements spreads. Merleau-Ponty, appealing to Goldstein's and Schilder's work,[1] shows one's experience of one's own body to be structured. The volume of the body's space has an inner postural axis, a dynamic figure which turns to and answers to correlates in the field about oneself. This postural axis gives one an integrated motor sense of the position of one's limbs, a practical sense such that for each shift in hand, torso, or leg the corresponding positions of the rest of the posture is given. And the line of dynamic tension of the postural diagram produces a "body image"—a quasi-visual sense of how one would look from the outside. On the other hand, the bodies of others normally appear to me as sustaining postures, elaborating positions, gaits, and gestures, confronting tasks, reaching for objectives—as my body so appears to them. I do not perceive the bodies of others as outlines delimiting colors and substance, but perceive them by their inner lines of posture and movement.

There is today a Gestaltist physiology that does not attempt to decompose behavior into elementary reflexes, but correlates typical chemical and electrical levels, sensory thresholds, positions, schematic and systematic mobilizations of the organism with a sensory environment articulated in patterns that have vital or practical significance for specific kinds of organisms. The motility of an organism both responds to and directs its sensibility. The older empiricism had sought to explain its positions and movements by correlating them with an environment defined in mathematical, physical, chemical, and electrical terms. This was not—could not be—justified by supposing that its sensibility is an apparatus to record the environment in the ways scientific observation and theory records and conceptualizes it. It was rather supported by the assumption that one could separate the pure facts, the givens, which can produce real effects on the material organism, from the significant patterns which would be imposed on the givens by the sensibility of the organism—meanings put on them by mental operations. The practice of this separation is as old as metaphysics—indeed, it is metaphysics. It has concealed the field and its patterns to which a living organism is sensitive and to which its motility responds. It has concealed the behavior and nature of an organism.

1. Sensuous Sense

When the organism in question is ourselves, we can describe what it is that we perceive. Phenomenology, Merleau-Ponty thought, showed what a metaphysic-free description of what is really given could be.

It is significant patterns and not atomic stimuli that an organism perceives and that its behaviors respond to. The "sensuous sense" of these patterns is not a conceptual meaning produced by mental or linguistic operations; it is incarnate in sensuous material. It is the cohesion, position, role with which a sensible thing becomes perceivable. It is the referentiality by which the sensuous elements of a lemon hold together as a unit and by which it contrasts with and fits in with its setting. It is the sense of a painting or a musical phrase, of a gesture, scowl, smile, or dance step. It is also that "gestural significance" linguistic expressions have, formed and conveyed in the vocalization. It is the meaning historical developments have—a sense that was not projected into them by the intentions of the historical actors or simply by the interpretative schemata of historiographers. Even in geometry the pure, ideal ideas emerge from an idealization of the round, the flat, the straight edge—of perceptually given morphological structures. Once the idealization is effected, it makes its repetition superfluous—and can structure a field of further idealizations. The geometrical ideas themselves are not simply constituted by mental acts, but emerge out of the physiognomy of the sensible; and they engender one another.

Everywhere this incarnate meaning is something that "emerges," rather than is constituted by a second mental operation on brute givens. There is a moment when individual events and feelings begin to take on a collective significance, a historical sense. There is a moment when the babbling of an infant becomes speech, when spots of color on canvas begin to mean something, when displacements of tissue and bone become gestures, when postures and attitudes take form at the confluence of chemical, electrical, and mechanical reactions. Merleau-Ponty wished to focus the attention of philosophical scrutiny on these moments. The nascent meaning begins in a conjuncture of contingencies; it assembles families of appearances as a style assembles the moves of a dancer or the texts of a writer. At a certain moment the passage of facts also begins to project ahead like an exigency; what congeals as a form functions as a matrix for variation. There are movements in the perceived sensuous medium that make what is posited veer into a dimension, make points become pivots, lines become axes, contours become schemata, lights function as levels, colors as punctuations. The sensuous material is not an identity simply located in a hic et nunc; a transcendence irreducibly belongs to it. If the sensuous medium holds together, it is not a pure flux of sensations but a field that has coherence, figures and background, patterns and planes; it is by virtue of the levels, dimensions, and horizons that the colors, tones, and textures themselves form. And the sensuous sense dissolves as the patterns in which it is formed disintegrate. "The whole

description of our landscape and the lines of our inner mono-
logue needs to be redone: colors, sounds, and things—like Van
Gogh's stars—are foci and radiations of being."[2]

The elements and aspects of a sensuous pattern confirm
antecedent patterns and form significant unities across the
moments; coherent and cohesive figures form on fields, contrast with and align themselves with other figures in the field;
the different sensorial fields interlock and the intersensorial
field of the moment and the day before with that of the moment and the day after. But the thing that is perceived to subsist through the consistency of the profiles it shows across
successive moments of time is always a presumptive identity;
it remains as contingent as the sensuous elements that compose it. The world that the consistent and concordant fields of
things form is not therefore doubtful or illusory—for it is the
very apparition of reality for us, and no more systematic representation we form out of elements drawn from it could be
more certain than it. But we do not possess this consistency
and coherence of the world as we possess that of a conceptual
system; we await it and observe it. Reality is for us always in
suspense, extended in horizons. The inconsistent, the incompatible, the insignificant, the illusory, are its own possibilities.
Reality is not posited before us like a universe of objectivity,
like a system of certainty or a presented truth; it exists, Merleau-Ponty wrote, in the interrogative mode, a field of allusions and horizons soliciting our questioning.

Sartre had built on a different conception of sense. He saw
all referentiality, all significance as determining phenomena
by marking out a segregation between what is and is given,
and what it is not. All determination, according to Spinoza's
formula, is negation. Sartre interpreted this to mean that the
discriminations and relationships we establish in the field of
phenomena have no positive reality of their own, add nothing
to what appears, only function to make what is appear. Of
themselves they are so much nothingness—shimmering of
nothingness which plays on the surface of being. The phenomenal matter and its form do not have the same reality—
they are separated with all the difference there is between
being and nothingness. And there are specific experiences—
dramatically explored in the novel *Nausea*—where all
significance is experienced as nothingness, leaving the brute

being as it is in itself to show through. Then it becomes clear that all this nothingness—discriminations, segregations, groupings, structurings, relationships—comes from us and nowise affects being as it is in itself—intact in its own nonsignifyingness, nonreferentiality, or absurdity. For Merleau-Ponty, the patterning, the structuring, the referentiality do not merely separate a given from what it is not; they positively posit it, give it its consistency, its constancy, its cohesion over time. An unformed phenomenon is imperceptible; perception, he writes, *is* a figure on a background.[3] If the sense of things and of the world is contingent, provisional, forming out of and dissolving back into non-sense, this does not reveal the subjective origin of all differentiation and the negative nature of all subjectivity. To imagine a ground of pure being in itself, utterly positive, posited beneath is still to represent an order of being, and this representation could not be more fundamental than the phenomenal reality presented. The vertiginous or nauseous moments in which we experience the contingency of the significance by which things and the panorama of reality hold together are still moments within the passage of phenomenal reality. Sartre's man of bad faith and inauthenticity is from the outset devoted not to the phenomenal world but to the ideal— the ideal synthesis of being and meaning, God, a sphere where the coherence and consistency of things would have the purely given character, the imperviousness, and self-sufficiency of brute being, in which the ways things are for-us would be also the way they are in-themselves. But this would be only a phenomenal field organized according to a logic of identity, and not an experience that would transcend the phenomenal condition of reality to its metaphysical ground. Sartre paradoxically has supposed that there are absolutely lucid moments of experience, those of vertigo and nausea, in which the format of being as it is in itself is revealed, and that those moments of epiphany gave its ideal to phenomenal experience as bad faith construes it. The authentic consciousness would recognize the contingency of all the systems the phenomenal things and the phenomenal world embody, would at each moment realize that all that is but so much shimmering of nothingness over a ground of being in itself it has caught sight of in those moments of nausea. For Merleau-

Ponty there is a very deep, metaphysical error involved in judging as nothingness this phenomenal shimmering of reality, for the alleged format of utterly positive being in itself divined at moments beneath it is in fact also a phenomenon, and owes its alleged positivity to the consistency and coherence of the fabric of phenomenal reality.

2. The Intentional Organism

The phenomenological inventory of the patterns of the phenomenal field leads to a new conception of the perceiving and motile organism. The objectified body of empiricist physiology and behavior theory was coordinated with an environment broken down into simple unpatterned stimuli defined solely by their physical, chemical, or electrical properties. But, once we recognize that the world as determined by the theoretical natural sciences is not the world as it is in itself, but a representation given to a certain usage of our sensory-motor and also conceptual apparatus, we can recognize that the vital behaviors of an organism have rather to be coordinated with the perceptual field as patterned practically and vitally for it.

Sartre had separated the significance of the phenomenal world from its brute being, and ascribed that significance to consciousness. Significance, nothing but determination, determination which is shimmering of nothingness, originates in consciousness, which is itself pure aiming-at-being which ceaselessly takes a distance from all being. Merleau-Ponty rather correlates the patterns that form in the perceptual field with attitudes, movements, postures, and gestures of the organism. And the organism is sensible, perceptible both for others and for itself; it has the same kind of ontological status as the field of sensible reality that surrounds it. This is not to argue, with Dr. Johnson, that the contours that pattern significant things in the perceptible field are more than shimmerings of nothingness because the body can take hold of them. The body is not a material ground that could guarantee the certainty of its objects. It has phenomenal reality, it shares the reality of the phenomenal world, which, we have argued,

is provisional and contingent; but no other representation of
being could relativize or discredit the ever-only-presumptive
phenomenal reality, since they all derive from it.

Perception is itself movement and action; it is not a simple
passive being imprinted with stimuli. To see something is to
see how to reach it; to perceive a real, that is, intersensorial
thing is to take up a stand before it and mobilize one's various
surfaces and organs upon it. Already to see one pattern and
not two monocular images is to focus one's two eyes; already
to see a green or orange is to move over it with an adductive or
abductive movement of the gaze. The agent body is the locus
of a continual formation of postural schemata, attitudes, and
gestures. These are intentional in the sense that the diagrams
of position and movement themselves relate to objectives.

As object-oriented, a gesture is a process whereby the present phase is affected by and adjusts itself to the future phase.
The hand that opens and moves is already adjusting itself to
the contours of the doorknob. The diagram of the gesture
forms in this contraction of time, this totality of positions
where each position is determined by the final position and by
all the others. The living organism is a substance where such a
Gestalt forming over time is possible.

Such intentionality becomes sensible within the organism
as its postural schema. The postural axis is a dynamic motor
whole by which the position of the fingers and the wrist at a
given moment adjusts to the positions of the forearm and up-
per arm and torso, as well as to the anticipated position on the
doorknob in front of it. It is the way the body positions itself
before its field and its tasks; when one lies down, disengaging
oneself from one's field of concerns, the sense of the layout of
one's limbs subsides. Posture is intentional in that it is
polarized in function of its objective; correlatively, the objective emerges in relief as a figure in the field of perception in
the measure that the body positions itself before it. The body
positions itself in function of vitally, practically, or aestheti-
cally significant patterns of the sensuous medium of the
world; correlatively, the patterns of the phenomenal field are
significant for the positions and moves of the body.

The green grass appears visible to a glance of a certain
focus, pace, and intensity, which admits of variations, and the
glance that sees it now has not emanated from a subjective

agent within that spontaneously determines its own acts. It has taken form by contracting one of the possible variants of a way of looking for which the grass appears green, and which it has picked up by turning to the grass and adjusting its surfaces and their movements to it. Each glance takes form as equivalent to, interchangeable with, any of a certain range of variants of itself, and it thus perceives a green visible in general. Every particular green emerges as a momentary concretion of a depth or dimension of green, which is not merely a correlate of this particular glance that makes it visible, and every glance takes form by varying a schema of visual movement, which I did not invent, but which emerged as part of that prepersonal pact with the sensible field which is the birth of a living body. My glance which forms as a variant of the range of glances for which this green is visible takes place among the glances of others, equivalent to and interchangeable with them. My eyes see as one sees, as eyes of flesh see.

The phenomenon of body image is a striking effect of this intentional correlation of body motility or internal organization with the exterior. As the axis of tension of a posture forms in a body, it produces a quasi-visual sense of itself, as though seen from without. By seating oneself at a desk, one has a sense of how one's legs and feet are positioned under the table alongside of the other visible things; one has a sense of how one looks from the outside. Although one's gait is for oneself a dynamic pattern, and one has never seen it (trying to observe it in mirrors always disconnects one from it and makes it clumsy and unnatural), still when one is shown projected on a screen a file of people walking in silhouette, one readily picks out oneself. Thus the postural organization not only stations and steers the body in function of outside objects, but gives it an experience of itself as viewed from the point of view of that exterior. It not only projects its forces into the outside field but also projects an image of itself in that field.

Intentionality means grasp of significant structures. Its reality does not, in Merleau-Ponty's thought, lead to positing a spontaneous consciousness that would engender atemporal structures of identity, generality, and organization and project them over insignificant, unorganized givens imprinted on the receptor surfaces of the body. The intentional arc traverses the body, making a future position determine already the present phase of movement, making each part adjust to the others and maintain a unitary balance, axis of thrust, and poise. And it makes a present position into a schema or model for subsequent variations—by glancing at the green grass one sees the range of ways oneself and others can see it, by giving a certain width and thrust to one's step one already establishes the schema for a gait, by contracting the rhythm with which to type in words, not letters, one has learned to type all possible words. The organism is the locus of this continual elaboration of schemata, where every particular generalizes, where a particular is not just a given posited in its coordinate p and moment t, but of itself relates to variants of itself at future moments and with correlates of itself in other sites. Intentionality is the animation of the organism; it is, Merleau-Ponty writes, a sensible substance making itself an exemplar.[4]

3. Erotic Sense

The circumscribing of the layout of the perceptual-practical field to which an organism responds, the recognition of the sensuous sense inherent in its patterns, and the perception of the intentional nature of the body's postures, gestures, and movements are necessary for an understanding of the libidinal body, libidinal behaviors, and their correlates. But the libidinal body is in fact not for Merleau-Ponty only an example of the new understanding of the body that phenomenology makes possible. Analysis of the libidinal body will be pivotal in his work, so that in his later writings the concept of erotic sense will function as a key for defining sensuous sense generally, and the concept of the body intentionality that is regulated by it will become the model about which his understanding of sensibility will be elaborated.

The sexual drive, which elaborates its effects across the sensibility, affectivity, and motility, as well as in the cognitive and representational functions, and which is weakened as they weaken or are impaired, is not simply the activation of a system of sensory-motor circuits in the genital apparatus; it is a structuring of the whole behavior of an organism. The libido is intelligible neither as a system of causal reactions nor as an instinct, but as an intentionality. It is released not by objective properties of stimuli, properties identifiable physico-chemically, but by their meaning, their erotic sense. Sexuality is not merely apprehension of meaning, to be sure; it is behavior, caresses, and orgasm—but the release of sexual behaviors depends on the emergence of a meaning-structure in a person, object, or environment.

The libido—converting the physiognomy of a body into a form addressed to the limbs and surfaces of my body, making of the contingent arrangement of an anatomy something necessary to me, derailing the gear about that body, reorienting implements to the caressing hand, destining even the scattering sunlight and shadows to genital contact, complicating rational and professional relationships with double meanings and innuendos by which they allude to the intimacy of orgasm—is the very passage from nonsense to sense. Libidinous intimacy is intentional—orientation to, exhibition of, sense.

What is this erotic significance of a person or a situation? It is not a concept apprehended intellectually, is not even a representation. It is the way a perceived pattern is structured so as to accentuate the erogenous zones on a body or their analogues in an environment. This accentuated pattern does not form a spectacle before the detached gaze; it answers immediately to kisses and caresses, to erotic gestures in the body that perceives it. It appears to, exists for, a body that contracts a libidinous attitude, that virtually or already embraces it, in the way the smoothness of the snow adheres to the body-axis and sway of the skier, or the sense of buoyancy to the motile rhythm of the diver.

4. The Libidinous Intention

Sartre, we have seen, made of perception a radically singular act; the objective experience another has of me is irremediably alien to me. The impossible telos of love and sexuality, of all human encounters, is the integration of the objectivity with which one exists for others into one's own experience of oneself. For Merleau-Ponty perception is anonymous, its postures and movements induced by objects which are not merely correlates of my own acts but visible to any of a range of like acts, perceptible in general. And from the first one's postural sense of oneself engenders an exteriorized body-image; to be seen is to be visible, is to give oneself the perception of being seen. The sense of being a sensible object is not experienced as an alienation of which the other is guilty, and which would invariably motivate all human relations to be projects of capture and subjugation.

Merleau-Ponty's phenomenology of perception had set out to free entirely the theory of intentionality from what was idealist in it; intentionality is no longer the self-conscious positing of ideal identity-terms with which to synthesize passively given sense-data. The sense organ actively apprehends the sensory pattern—to see the green or the orange the eye focuses and moves across it with a specific rhythm, and is supported by the body's posture. If the visual data, the tones, textures, and odors are all combined into one perceptual thing, they are so combined by the body, inasmuch as its surfaces and organs form one system, inasmuch as it experiences what touches one surface as having an equivalent on other surfaces. There is correspondence between the textures and patterns of the outside things and the diagrams of position and apprehension in one's postural schema. The erotic sense in the position of someone perceived is the way this pattern, seen by one's eyes, has, within one's body, its immediate equivalent for one's touch, one's embrace. One "understands" the erotic sense of the other's position with the corresponding possibilities of one's own body schema. The infant, without the sensory-motor coordination apt to effect sexual actions, does not understand the adult copulation he witnesses in the bedroom, but perceives it as aggression. The grasp of the sense is seated in a correspondence or equivalence between a corporeal position perceived and one's inner postural axis.

Perception also involves a correspondence and equivalence between one's own exterior and one's interior. The postural axis, a felt dynamic schema, is accompanied by a "body image," a sense of what that position looks like from the outside. The body contracts its posture by addressing the outside layout, and in contracting the postural axis it also engenders a sense of its own exterior, it inserts itself in the panorama of the visible.

The sensitive body, then, is the locus of these two equivalencies. It is with one's own upright posture that one perceives the verticality of the pines, and it is with one's own supine and orgasmic postures that one perceives the lovemaking of others. One perceives the forms and positions of others, and also of exterior things, with one's own inner axes. And to perceive one's own axis of force inside is to perceive it as outside. One also does not perceive the outlines of another's body without perceiving its inner lines of force and movement. One's body sees its exterior by feeling its inner axes— and feels the inner axes of another body by seeing its exterior.

To say that the body's positions and moves are intentional now means that the body contracts an inner diagram of coordinated position when it perceives a figure outside; it is with its own intra-sensitive postural coordination that it knows the cohesion of an outside pattern. To say that an agent has a reflective awareness of himself or herself means that his or her inner diagrams of position and movement produce an immediate, exteriorized, quasi-visual version of themselves. Perception is an inscription of a dynamic version of the outside within and a reflection of oneself on the outside.

This analysis is most clear when conducted on sexual behavior. To see someone sprawled on the bed as seductive is to feel, forming within oneself, the movements of taking him or her. The other is structured perceptibly as a surface destined for kisses and embraces, the exterior relief of one's inward lines of feeling. The immediate appropriation of this exterior figure by one's own inner axes extends the appropriation with which one's own right hand conforms with and identifies with one's left hand as it goes to touch it, the appropriation with which one's interior identifies with one's own exterior form. And an inner axis of position or movement produces a body image; as one contracts a dynamic line of position one senses how one is exposed to an exterior view. The more intense one's sense of one's hovering or advancing motility is, the more intense is one's sense of one's obtrusiveness in exterior space, one's sense of the surface one turns to the advances of the other. Here self-consciousness is a demand for the kisses and caresses of another. In sexual experience what exposes itself outside of oneself afflicts and captivates; and, conversely, the more active one becomes, the more one becomes surfaces and substance supinely demanding the hold and palpations of the other.

Sexual behavior is, Merleau-Ponty said, an experience of the metaphysical structure of our flesh.[5] The libido is seated in the structure of sensibility. A body that has sense organs is also inevitably a body that desires libidinally; here esthesiology is prolonged into a theory of the libidinal body.[6] Or rather, the reverse is the case: Merleau-Ponty's later conception of the process of perception builds on and generalizes his analysis of erotic sensibility. The sense of sensible things is not the set of their invariant traits disengaged by a play of imagination but their inner physiognomies; it is with our inner body-axis that we capture the inner diagrams of the chair, the table, and the pine tree. All sense perception involves something like a carnal embrace, and in *The Visible and the Invisible* Merleau-Ponty will invoke *flesh* to designate all sensible reality. The reflexivity involved in this intentional coordination with an exterior figure is the production of a body-image by every position we take and move we make; it is not the transparency of self-consciousness. To perceive is to become perceptible, even for oneself, to insert oneself as a quasi-visual pattern into the field one looks into. Intentionality is not foray and capture only, it is exposure. Merleau-Ponty liked to quote writers who when they went to contemplate nature wrote about a sense of being seen by the trees and the clouds they looked at.

5. *The Erotic Appropriation of Time*

The libido—a general term. It would name the instincts and purposes of the genus pursuing, in our mortal lives, the immortality of the race. Yet what in our lives is more personal than our sexual tastes, and the immanent satisfaction or pleasure into which we relapse when our unutterably individual craving is consummated? Of all the women and men that pass, it is finally just *this one*, this particular combination of traits, that triggers our erotic feeling, that answers to the singular nature of our lust. The psychoanalyst who tracks down the itinerary of our erotic adventures and misadventures is indeed delineating what is individual in our person, is drawing the portrait of that person I am, who does not subsist like a substance but exists like the plot of a history. If the events of my mental life and those of my social and professional life do not simply make me a participant in, a part of, universal reason or universal discourse or the community, is it not because they are also fitted into the ways and byways of that irreducibly individual thread of history that is spun by the libidinous impulses in me? To each erotic encounter I bring all my infantile obsessions, and because I crave only mortal flesh and blood each rendezvous is an assignation with death.

The events of our erotic life, then, do not simply succeed one another and pass like the events of nature, nor even build on one another like events of a biological evolution. Each repeats the drama of our birth and anticipates our dying; they would be historical in the strongest—the Heideggerian—sense. As the level at which life in me assumes an individual configuration, where my existence is always still infantile and already dying, where gropingly my life has simultaneously to discover and to invent its own itinerary and destiny, as the level where the universal meaning of my mental operations and the social meaning of my practical initiatives also take on an irreducibly individual sense, is not my erotic life the very level at which authenticity, individuality, takes form? Is not the libido the natural material out of which an individual history is elaborated, out of which my person, my existence in the first person singular, is formed?

But, as an individual rises into relief on the levels of a field, and as an individual glance forms by varying a schema of vision instituted in the postural schema of the body, so one's own personal existence forms as a variant on schemas of existence maintained in the anonymous adjustment of one's sensibility and motility to the world in general. Every singular act of which it is made schematizes itself as it passes, turns into a schema open to variations.

The sexual embrace can then have this sense of being an experience of the metaphysical structure of corporeality because we risk abjection and invest all our brazenness and all we can dare in it, because this man or this woman loom as figures of the original man or woman of our infancy and of all the subsequent men and women, because these escapist gestures and cravings for solitude and night, or these convulsive denudings and profanations are but crests on a wave formed by the whole force of a style of life, because infantile anxieties still and mortal terrors agitate these feelings. Here is that structure of anonymity, *l'on primordial* which Merleau-Ponty said "has its own kind of authenticity, and never ceases, and sustains the great passions of the adult."[7] If the erotic passion is one of these great passions, is indeed the great passion, it is because here more than anywhere it is the infant I was, the pure body, the cadaver I will become, it is anyone, everyone, that craves and feels in me, is prostrate and abject, triumphs idolatrously in my flesh.

In Freudian terminology, the libidinal history is a history not of continuities and evolutions but of complexes, traumata, and fixations, and of the crises that produce these fixations and break them. The fixation is produced not by some sort of inertia or reification of a behavior that will not pass and keeps getting recycled; it is produced by the way a particular present response comes to schematize itself, the way an erotically charged figure comes to count for all men and all women, the way a given situation comes to prolong itself into dimensions within which subsequent encounters will take form. This passing into an anonymous mode functions positively to make possible a singular act and its sense, for an act of a body is always a figure produced by variation on a schema. The general schema is what gives its sense, its direction, its relatedness with all that has come to pass and all that is to come, to the singular impulse; it is what gives their urgency and their necessity to contingencies of anatomy and chance encounters. It is also the relapse of an encounter with an alien and singular being into a relationship with only the general form of corporeality, the denouement of an individual drama into a predicament in which one is held.

This relationship between the particular and the schematic, so keenly felt in all our passionate experiences, also gives us insight into the character of all our motility. It is by contracting general schemata, which persist and focus and frame our practical and perceptual fields, that singular acts— divergencies on schemata—become possible. And every singular act generalizes, becomes a schema, becomes anonymous. Our behaviors form in this alternation of the singular and the schematic, as our perception opens from time to time on the singular relief of a situation standing out from the general lines of the world with which we generally content ourselves.

6. The Hypotheses of the Phenomenological Description

Sartre, we complained, did not explicate orgasmic behavior, but only decomposed it into manipulations and pleasures. Merleau-Ponty's more discerning exposition contains an analysis of libidinous behavior, and this analysis enables him to explain in new terms the intentionality and the reflexivity involved in all sensory-motor behavior. Yet the essential concepts that govern his account of libidinal existence originate outside this sphere—in perception and in praxis.

It is striking that the only feeling Merleau-Ponty brings up in his work is libidinous sensuality. The stated goal of the text he wrote on sexuality in *Phenomenology of Perception* is to show how objects and the world come to exist for us through affectivity.[8] Yet nowhere does he speak of what makes sexual behavior voluptuous—only of what makes it meaningful, only of the libido as the force that makes of the successive events of life a personal history. But in the intentional structure of erotic desire, its object-relatedness is singularly inseparable from affectivity; what is voluptuous is the erotic trouble and craving, the intention itself. It is pleasurable torment, which does not seek to put an end to itself, does not seek an end for itself. Have we not already deformed it by conceiving it in teleological terms? It does not know what it seeks and does not seek a term; it is exasperation, agitation, that provokes itself always more.

Seeking the locus of the breakdown of sexual competence in Goldstein's patient Schneider, Merleau-Ponty posited, beyond the operations of the sensory-motor circuits, the structuring capacities of perception, imagination, and representation, an inner diaphragm that determines the scope of what makes sense to that life, an intentional arc that bears the body with all its organs toward the world and which would be libido. But is the libido really to be equated with the teleological movement that makes the parts of the body hold together as a posture, integrates these sensory-motor cycles, makes these organs one organism? Does not the orgasmic body figure as a body decomposed, dismembered, dissolute, where postures and dynamic axes form and deform in the limp indecisiveness of the erotic trouble? Is it not a breaking down into a mass of exposed organs, secretions, striated muscles, systems turning into pulp and susceptibility? The orgasmic body is not the body regressing to a state prior to that of the organism it became when it was able to contract posture, mobilize itself, work and exteriorize a relationship with exteriority, when it contracted gestures and expression—but the body drifting toward a state on the far side of organization and sense, a state where action loses its seriousness and becomes play, where equivocal gestures and suggestive linguistic formulations accumulate double meanings, allusions, innuendos, are no longer indicative but teasing and provocative, breaking up into nonsense and laughter by excess. Dissolute impulses not constitutive of sense but productive of phantasms.

Merleau-Ponty wrote that the Freudian unconscious is in fact not a second order of representational consciousness but a sensible consciousness. Not constitutive of a second system of representations, but locus of emergence of incarnate meaning. But a Freudian would answer that this interpretation does not take into account the contradiction between consciousness and the unconscious. Is it not rather that the libido is the locus, not of sense at all, but of what is unavowable?

The phenomenology of perception shows how the perceived object is never present, nor even presentified, represented, but is always only sketched out in advance, presumed. The objects of representational consciousness are then in fact objectives, and to perceive something is to begin to project dealings with it. The perceived structure is a matrix of possible perceptions, and the representational faculty, when taken as an intentionality, is open upon the future, becomes projective, becomes the faculty for the possible. The intention in perception assembles, poises, mobilizes the sensibility as an advance-hold, a *Vorhabe,* a *prise,* an *I can.*

There is indeed a representational faculty involved in the libido, but is it really this sort of hold on the possible? Is it not rather essential to passion that it not straightforwardly represent its objective? Passion can suffer neither the pleasure nor a child being posited as objectives. If erotic desire can be conceived as a modality of consciousness of something, what it is turned to are phantasms, objects of consciousness that cannot really be objectives, that are impossible. Is there not here a specific kind of relationship with the future that is not a hold on the possible but a being held by the impossible—which alone could account for the essentially exasperated nature of voluptuous feelings? And which would explain why the relationship with this form of object, with this future, is not effected in a posture or stance or hold, in a modality of postural mobilization, but in the spasmodic cravings of orgasm?

Does not this relationship with an impossible future indicate how singular is the time-structure of the life the libido elaborates? Freud brought out the ahistorical, immemorial nature of the Id—the timelessness of the unconscious. Here the past does not pass on, nor does it really come to pass; it is not something accomplished. Here the infant each of us had to begin by being subsists, intact, still infantile. The movements of the orgasmic body are no longer expressive, the kissing mouth *in-fans*, no longer forming speech, regressing to infantile orality. Every erotic game one engages in works again at some infantile drama. Is not all that is mortifying in psychoanalysis this teaching that one never gets any further, that one is still a jealous baby, that orgasm, when it is really lustful and passionate, is this reversion? Rather than historical moments in which the sense of a whole existence is instituted, are not the moments of orgasm almost the reverse—essentially mortifying moments of birth, where nothing any longer is strung out between birth and death as a line of sense or a project? Rather than the itinerary of a destiny projecting its vector of sense to its own end, is not the time of the libido rather a time of complexifications, fixations, traumata, regressions, crises—a zigzag time that suddenly shorts out between birth and death?

Shorts out on contact with alterity. Are not the paroxysms of voluptuous sensuality made of a sensibility that finds in the embrace with what is most akin that which is unutterably strange? Do not the erotic phantasms proliferate in the region of this impossible alterity?

3.

Phenomenology of the Face and Carnal Intimacy

1. The Face

In the phenomenology of Emmanuel Levinas the erotic body is described by contrast with the expressive body. But the central theme of Levinas's elaboration of the body as expressive organism is not, as in Merleau-Ponty, the teleologically significant gesture; it is the face. Levinas emphasizes not expression in its indicative or informative function, speech as communication, but expression in its vocative and imperative force. Communication is articulated in questions and responses, appeals and demands. Appealing and ordering are behaviors of a body—that faces.

When a face faces me, it shows color, shape, and relief; it exhibits density and elasticity, solidity and weight. It is like a surface with which any sensible object spreads out in the light and becomes a phenomenon. The surface does not become a face when we take its shape and movements as signs. In facing me someone is not giving me signs of what is in his mind. In facing me someone greets me, summons my attention, indicates something in the world that is open to me too, answers my call, exposes himself to me, contests me.

In his face the other is other. He manifests himself as different by exposing thoughts I could not have conceived or foreseen, by understanding thoughts I present to him in ways sur-

58

prising to me, by responding with an urgency, an irritation that puzzles me, disturbs me, delights me. But he shows himself as other in addressing me, calling upon me, appealing to me, and in contesting me, judging me, assenting to me.

The other affirms his otherness in his inalienable power to contest my interpretation—my interpretation of the world about me into which he comes, or my interpretation of his voice. Turning of himself to face me, the other determines the sense of his presence. In his movement of contestation he reopens the interval between me (and all my representations of him) and himself; he rises always beyond whatever I have comprehended and apprehended of him. He withdraws into his separation, into his absence, into the silence from which he came.

Expression is vocative: with a glance, a word, a gesture, someone greets me, appeals to me, invokes me. The first move with which someone faces me calls upon me, and each act with which information can be exchanged also addresses me and calls for a response. And in facing me, the other questions me, contests me, makes demands on me. Even if his glance is light, if his voice hardly stirs the air, if his gestures refrain from touching me, his expression has imperative force. In responding to another who faces me I have already recognized the other's right to question me, have recognized authority and sovereignty. A face is the place where poverty and nakedness and also magisterium break out in the sufficiency and serviceability of the surfaces of things.

The other faces in the nakedness of eyes that do not shine, but appeal; in the bare voice, which is not an instrument but the way to come disarmed and disarming; in gestures, which is the way to approach empty-handed.[1] This way of turning to me the most liquid and vulnerable surfaces, this way of touching me with only a vibration that dies away, which I can resist by doing nothing at all, by doing whatever I was doing, this way of advancing while holding back one's weight and force, this way of coming just to speak, is the way of coming naked, disarmed, and poor. This way of approaching, with only a glance, a word, a gesture, calls upon me, addresses an appeal to me.

This approach signals to me, this exposure solicits me. The other singles me out, singularizes my existence, calls up an I.

The one who faces me requires something of me, and requires first that I answer him in the first person singular, that I answer in my own name, that I be I. To answer to the appeal of another is to rise in an existence in the first person, a source and a resource unto itself.

But a question is a demand, an invocation, a summons. The other who appeals to me in the destitution of his face also rises before me in height, in sovereignty. In facing, the other contests my perspective, puts my interpretation into question, makes demands on me. The capability of facing me is a power to require responsibility of me and demand justification. Although his look comes from without it is imperative; although his voice is disarming it is urgent; although his hands refrain from touching or taking hold their solicitation is pressing.

To turn to another who faces is to expose oneself to judgment. This is understood when a greeting is acknowledged. An understanding of the vocative and imperative force of a face is always presupposed in the understanding of the indicative forms of its expression. To agree to speak, to answer another's greeting, to enter into conversation, is to agree to be judged. It is to admit the other's right to question me, make demands on me, require of me my presence and the presentation to him of my goods and my world. The one who faces always requires something of me; he first requires that I answer in my own name. I find myself, my existence in the first person singular, as an obligation. I may, to be sure, endeavor to deceive the other, evade his summons; I may endeavor to seduce my judge, refuse his question. Existence as an I is a possibility for ruse and lies. These are possible only because the very approach of the other does contest me and subject me to judgment.

2. The Carnal Body

Sexuality is addressed to somebody in his or her carnality. What is this specifically carnal format of the other? Neither Sartre's nor Merleau-Ponty's phenomenology has circumscribed its essence. For Sartre the carnal is the ideal synthesis of alien subjectivity with objectivity, produced by disconnecting a body first perceived actively and instrumentally, in such a way that the intentions of the alien subjectivity are sensed to go no further than feeling the surfaces of his or her own objectivity being caressed and embraced. But the synthesis is ideal rather than phenomenal, and dissipates before the orgasmic agitation that strives to penetrate it. Merleau-Ponty defines the libidinal body as one in which erogenous zones are accented and immediately addressed to one's own motor possibilities. The carnal is a sensuously significant structure of the perceptible body. Flesh for Merleau-Ponty is connective tissue rather than substance.[2] Yet what makes up the immediacy, the obsessive force of this presence? In his phenomenology of the face, Levinas shows how the vocative and imperative force of expression are *phenomena*—that is, are perceived (and not simply posited by interpretation or hypothesis) in the facing another does with the nakedness of his eyes, with the disarming contact of his voice, with his empty-handed gestures. In his phenomenology of the carnal, Levinas endeavors to delineate the *phenomenon* of the carnal and the way it becomes perceptible in the erotic denuding.

Eroticization is something that happens to a body already expressive, a body that faces. It occurs in an exhibitionist denuding, a divesting not only of apparel and gear, but of form, function, and meaning.[3] Of course, someone cannot denude himself or herself without the light and the shadow molding the nudity and giving it form. But the carnal body does not hold its form; the erotic position is shifting and uncertain, is not a posture or an attitude. Its agitation is made of a continual formation and dissolve of poses. Unlike the laborer who bares her arms, or the dancer who exhibits his rebus torso, the erotically denuded one is nonfunctional, gratuitous, and vulnerable in the midst of things.

In the face nakedness is significant; the eyes, exposed and vulnerable, appeal, speak out: the voice, disarmed and disarming, queries and directs; the hands, empty-handed, inform and indicate, beckon and order. The erotic nudity is equivocal. It is the nudity of a being that throws itself into the light without elucidating anything, uncovers itself without disclosing anything. Its glances double with allusions and teasing, its words with shifting meanings, its movements tremble with innuendo. In this proliferation of suggestiveness responsibility collapses; the face clouds over with confusion and ardor.

The carnal is vulnerable in the midst of things, finds itself without resistance or will. It is other with an alterity that is that of an existence exposed to the dangers of the world, that is there by chance and gratuitously, that appeals for tenderness and care. Yet this vulnerability is also insistent, enslaving. It is not only the language that speaks of the erotic that is equivocal, that says what it means by innuendo, double-meanings, improper usages of words; the carnal itself appears in the equivocation of vulnerability and exorbitant materiality, and it has become formless, nonfunctional, uninformative by excess. It is not that an expressive organism was reduced to insignificance, its glances losing their appeal and their authority, its words their sense, its gestures becoming spasms of matter. The whole body denuded addresses one now with multiple and contradictory appeals and demands, no longer invoking from a distance but giving itself over in provocation. Its utterances have not become devoid of significance, but accumulate meanings behind meanings, fragment in all directions, the confluence of incompatible meanings breaking up in laughter. Hands that freed themselves from holding in order to speak now free the whole body, appealing for everything and for nothing, lewd and wanton. The authority that shone in the face is not abolished but compromises itself, making exorbitant claims and demands on one, playing with its power over one, no longer contesting one only but holding one captive in an irresponsible and inconstant sovereignty without seriousness. In taking off clothing, the denuding does not reduce the uniforms of socially comprehensible roles to the simplicity of biological functions, but contaminates even apparel and gear with equivocal usages.

Is it not the indecisive and equivocal carnality, rather than the splendor of proportions not yet disfigured by the fatigue of years, that makes youth troubling? Classical beauty consisted in the splendor of measure, harmony, and order; such is the face of someone whose inner equilibrium and symmetrical contours seem to secure it against death—for one "looking," in Yeats's words, "for the face I had before the world was made." Plato's *Symposium* concludes that the erotic impulse orients the life whose spirituality is devoted to order, to beauty, and consequently to eternity—and that the ultimate eros is philosophical. Yet is it not the indecisive carnal substance not held in resolved forms that makes the awkward youth so troubling? And as the imminence of death engraves its ravages more and more tangibly on a face, giving to each aging visage a material disorder all its own, wrinkles and folds shadowing a complexion with unsettled tones, this materiality more and more palpable denudes one who had armored himself or herself with measure, harmony, and order against passion. We love the intimations of immortality with a metaphysical love, whose joy wills eternity, but carnal love cherishes mortal flesh and blood.

3. Libidinal Desire

The libidinal response is neither a drive nor an instinct; it is provoked by the exhibition of the carnal. But Levinas thinks Merleau-Ponty was wrong to conceive of the libidinal impulse with the phenomenological concept of intentionality, however reconstructed—to be concerned with the carnal is not to grasp a sense. He thinks that Sartre was wrong to conceive of it as an appropriative project: the caress is not an action giving form, molding material with spirit, nor is it a grasping in order to reduce the alterity of the other. Levinas conceives of erotic desire with the existential concept of *care* elaborated by Heidegger.[4]

For Heidegger the first "object" of our awareness is the void of death; we know our being because we sense the abysses of nothingness that menace it; we know any being as such because we sense the confines of nonbeing ahead, before which a world appears. The sense of death, of nothingness, is anxiety. The sense we have of our own existence is a care for our being in the world, because we are anxious about the nothingness that threatens it. Anxiety is a recoil before the oncoming nothingness which posits and cleaves to one's own being. It can be fled or reversed; one can also set forth one's positive being as destined for nothingness, in sacrifice and in the resolute living out of one's ex-istence.

To be troubled erotically is to be concerned about someone, to be solicitous for someone. To love someone carnally is to see the infant in the man or woman; it is to be anxious for mortal flesh and blood. It is to relate oneself with the other in such a way that one experiences one's existence as a harbor for another. To care for someone carnally is to feel one's own substance to be a haven against the death sensed imminent in the carnal nudity of another. But, unlike care in Heidegger, the erotic care is a voluptuous sense, obvious of itself. The erotic tenderness is like a compassion, but not a practical concern that aims to heal; it goes to join the vulnerability and weakness of the one it addresses—complacent compassion.

This care, tender and anxious, is also equivocally violent and profaning.[5] It finds itself solicited by a presence wanton and exhibitionist, no longer appealing only but inciting, no longer contesting and judging but demanding amoral complicity. The erotic tenderness is rash and shameless, before a non-public existence uncovered without being disclosed, exposed without anything being understood or communicated. The denuding of the carnal does not have the character of a project but of a profanation—a secrecy violated without being divulged.

Caresses are the movements of tenderness and profanation. The hand that caresses is not exploring, not collecting tangible impressions or following out a meaning. Despite Merleau-Ponty's insistence, the carnal does not offer any significant structure for the caress to grasp; the caress is not really a gesture. It is also not acting, not moving to bring out a possibility, attain an objective, is not forming or molding. It does not realize an appropriation; it returns obsessively over the surface fondled, as over ever-virgin territory. The caress moves without knowing what it wants or what it is doing. The hand that caresses, limp and passive, is without will, without program.

Is it then, as Sartre says, a stratagem designed to fascinate another subjectivity with its incomprehensible patterns, its disconcerting nakedness, so as to obtain from the other assent to a will that does not communicate itself? Do its maneuvers aim to hold the alien subjectivity on its own surfaces, making it lose sight of its goals, tasks and projects, disarming the alien subjectivity? But an alien will can be overcome by stratagem only because ruse dissimulates itself as passion.

And what turns into erotic passion is not the anxiety that senses itself threatened by an inapprehendable exterior will; it is an anxiousness of vulnerable and will-less carnal nature.

What provokes the erotic passion is the other denuding himself or herself without knowing what he or she is doing, or why, not exercising sovereignty of will but entangled in dreams and fantasies, a will breaking down into nonsense and laughter. The carnal does not ensnare like a will teeming with designs, but afflicts as an irresponsibility that has to be cared for. What excites the voluptuous impulse is not an alien freedom captured, objectified, but this freedom untamed—not a freedom resolute and responsible but animal freedom in the tumult of caprice and sensuality. It is by force and intelligence that an alien will could be resisted; the caress is weakness, troubled and tender; it is movements that do not parry the exorbitant presence that invades, movements that subdue nothing, that do not possess, that are possessed. Lustful movements are repetitions, divagations, a foundering. One finds oneself in erotic trouble as in a dream having forgotten why one came here or where one is going or what one sought to obtain by passing this way.

The erotic voluptousness is not simply an extreme degree in intensity of pleasure and contentment. Its movements make contact with a plenitude of content, to be sure; but in the silk of skin, the warmth of down, the liquid continuity of contours gratifying the touch that conforms to them, something else is divined—the alterity of the other in the guise of passivity and susceptibility, ripples of torment and pleasure that die away in the exposed substance. Voluptuous sensuality craves to join, to feel as concordance and pleasure, the alien in another's pleasure. The sensitivity that quickens erotic agitation is not a clairvoyance that assembles the parts and phases of movement to converge upon an objective; it is a sensuality that fills with itself yet is never contented with itself, feeds on itself in an ever-augmenting hunger. It is tormented and exasperated by its very pleasure, pleasure over the pleasure of one irreducibly alien. Voluptuous sensuality does not look to put an end to its torment but abandons itself to it, a craving that voluptuously craves its craving.

Erotic craving is not to be assimilated to need or to a desire for being. Here pleasure is not a contentment that stabilizes, but excitement that torments itself. And the voluptuous craving is not a desire that strives to fix or posit itself in being, to sculpture a statuesque version of itself. It is anarchical, excited by its own spasms. It does not strive toward the higher inertia of the poetic, toward a rhetorical form of its quest, but moves as a descent into a Shakespearean underworld, where the quest reverberates in the labyrinth of sorcerers' innuendo and derision. Erotic movements are agitations that do not know what to do with the exorbitance of what one holds in one's hands, agitations of an exposure that seeks ever more susceptibility.

4. Carnal Intimacy, and Its Time

Husserl took as evident that presence is the telos of all consciousness; all consciousness aims at the presence of being. For Sartre erotic intimacy achieves appropriation; the elusive omnipresent alien subjectivity has been captured in an objective form whose contours subject it to one's powers. For Merleau-Ponty carnal intimacy is the locus of emergence of sense. The inner configuration of the other is captured in one's corporeal axes, and one's own dynamic diagram is exposed in palpable reality. This moment gives a personal sense to the anonymity of the rest of my time; my hours as a speaker of discourse intelligible to anyone, my days as laborer in the public productive apparatus, my years as functionary in a profession have, in addition to their anonymous meaning, an individual sense inasmuch as they also converge on the moments of erotic intimacy. The personal sense of my expressive, practical, professional, public life is elaborated in the movements of sensual intimacy.

Erotic sensuality clouds the horizons that external perception establishes; erotic moves do not extend distances but, Levinas writes, are moved by obsessive contact.[6] Lust is not able to maintain its distances from what touches it; in the mind clouded with sensuality everything is disordered and out of perspective. Erotic intimacy is contact with the alien itself; it is not a presence of a form whose sense has been assimilated, nor is it the practical closeness of what is in one's hands or within reach, nor is it the haunting presence of what affects our moods from afar.

The sensual embrace is not comprehensive or comprehending. Cognition keeps itself close to what touches it through memory; serious knowledge is knowledge of the facts—the *factum*, the past. What is present to the understanding is represented; all cognition is retrospective. The erotic contact was not given in an advance representation; it is a *factum*, one's trouble is what has come to pass without one's having given it to oneself. One lives this contact without perspectives, without a future.

Tenderness moves in this space with moves moved by the other, moving only to expose themselves the more. It has no horizons but this insatiable contact. Erotic intimacy is closeness without prospects, closeness for the sake of closeness.[7] The voluptuous affliction is a complicity between two vulnerable and mortal ones, two dissolute ones, a complicity in view of nothing, or rather for the sake of this intimacy more inward than every frankness and every insincerity. It is a complicity that the misunderstandings of lovers do not disintegrate, as it was not established by their understanding one another.

Carnal intimacy is not a practical space; it does not open a field for action. The erotic movements are agitation that handles and fondles without keeping anything in its place, without extending its force outward and without going anywhere. Here nothing will be accomplished; one will waste time, unprofitably. Voluptuousness has no tasks and no objectives and leaves no heritage; after all the caresses and embraces, the carnal is left intact, virgin territory. When lovers meet, their pleasure has neither practical nor social horizons; their intimacy closes itself off against society. Nothing is to be learned from listening to lovers' talk. Its formulations are not informative, it is not even evocative—words that tease and complain without any sense of sincerity.[8] Its order lacks imperative force, does not command, cannot make judgments; it provokes anything at all and assents to anything, even when it says no and never and only if. It is not the locus from which would emerge the meaning of one's history.

For Levinas erotic intimacy is not the locus where the assimilation of what is irreducibly other is attempted or achieved; it is on the contrary a presence of what is irreducibly remote, contact with what can never be present or represented, tangency to the other without intermediaries. In this sense erotic intimacy reveals the metaphysical structure of our existence. For Levinas to interpret life existentially (as existence or ex-stasis, standing outside itself) or intentionally (as aiming for what is transcendent to it) is to interpret it not as a project to assimilate every other, to reduce all alterity to identity, but as longing for the remote, fascination with what remains other. Erotic voluptuousness would then be the moment and erotic intimacy the place where contact with the other in his or her vulnerability, mortality, insecurity in the layout of the world, in his or her agitation without projects and expressivity irremediably equivocal, in his or her gratuity—where the contact with the other in all the evidence of alterity—becomes voluptuous enjoyment.

As craving, longing in the very intensity of voluptuous pleasure, erotic desire thrusts itself into the darkness and surprise of futurity. The strange state which Levinas identified as the frailty and vulnerability by which the carnal is other, and solicits, is also a strange future. The carnal is dissimulation, all conceits and artifices. That toward which desire casts itself is not represented in advance by the clairvoyance of an intention, is not apprehended by a power that will force the possible into being. Erotic agitation is not any kind of enterprise or project; it advances upon what is not possible for it.[9]

Voluptuous abandon interrupts the time of one's own project and destiny and does not open upon the project and destiny of a historical epoch or a generation. It opens rather upon the unendingly recommencing time of fecundity—the existential structure at the base of the idea of infinity.

5. Existence and Fecundity

Ex-istence, as existential philosophy understands this concept, is a movement; it is that by which our being is oriented to what is other than itself. It is simultaneously a movement out of one's own given or present state of being. Erotic intimacy is for Levinas the most intense form of being oriented to alterity, without return, without reflective recuperation, without assimilation or appropriation. Fecundity is for him the strongest movement of existence out of itself, out of one's own identity. For it is one's own existence moving into another identity.

A child derives not only its physico-chemical material from its parents but also its existence as care in the world, and its very identity. My child, Levinas writes, is not only mine as a work or a creation is mine; its existence is not only an effect or a product of my existence but is my own existence now discontinuous from me, become other. Self-appropriation and self-maintenance is not the universal theme with which the movement of our existence is to be conceived.

Levinas of course does not put into erotic desire the biological finality of reproduction. Fecundity is not realized in the sphere of desires and projects; no action which would give form could give existence. Through its fecundity an existence is transported by its own constitutive thrust outside itself entirely, into a new time without any synthetic bond with the past it had accumulated and the future its powers open. Here transcendence without return, without immanence, desire without satisfaction, becomes transubstantiation.[10] In fact the erotic transport already effects a deliverance from one's identity, one's destiny and responsibility. In voluptuous passion one's sensibility moves to support and complacently sustain the pleasure and the torment of the other whose visage is effaced in carnal ardor. In the midst of this ex-perience, experience oblivious of oneself, abandoned to the other, the discontinuity of fecundity, in which one's existence comes to exist with another identity, is realized.

Through fecundity one's time recommences in an absolute future that was nowise in potency, nowise in the present. In my child my existence recommences, restored to all the possibilities it had determined and resolved, delivered of all that has come to pass, has become definitive and irrevocable for it, delivered of the guilt of all it had committed—pardoned.[11] This recommencement of a process of time delivered of its own past, this projection of a new itinerary of time across a discontinuity of identity that delivers it from the passive synthesis of aging, diagrams a coordinate of infinite time.

Infinite time is not eternity, equivalent to a present that would be nothing but present, neither passing nor implicating anything still unresolved. But the spontaneity or ecstatic projection in existence does not produce infinite time. A projection of existence can be determinate only because it projects itself toward termini that determine it, and because it retains these determinations, is encumbered by its own initiatives. For Heidegger, the concept of infinite time is the abstract structure of a life structured as day-after-day, structured in units of time of the same form, in which recommences always the same content of tasks. One forms each day's content as a recurrence of the prior day, and deals with the tasks of each day in such a way as to expect their recurrence the next day—in order to forget or flee the end of one's time. Practical life thus forms its activities along an axis of an unending succession of days, each equivalent. For Levinas the denuding of the carnal dissipates this practical forgetting or fleeing of mortality. And in the oblivion of self in erotic experience, fecundity brings about a recommencement of one's existence in another trajectory of time. Only fecundity could give a real existential basis to an infinity of time.

Across the discontinuity of existence which fecundity effects, there is a relationship that is constitutive of existence as parental and as infantile. Parental existence consists in carnal care for the child, a relationship of the existence with itself, since the child exists with the existence of the parents. Yet such care is not self-appropriation—for in the tender and voluptuous care of the parents for the child the infantile identity first arises. The infantile existence does not come to exist for itself, with its own identity, by a spontaneous recoil of its life back upon itself. In fact the movement of existence opens a being to what is outside of itself, and its return upon itself is reflected back from that outside. It is in finding itself sustained and supported by the sensuous element of the world that a life enjoys living, enjoys itself, forms as an ipseity. But before infantile existence acquires an identity for itself in the enjoyment of the sensible elements it acquires identity in the sensual enjoyment of parental love. Infantile life first acquires a sense of itself, identifies itself, in finding itself sustained and supported by the sensuous element of parental care. Scheler, in a famous essay,[12] argued that love—as hatred—is a relationship not with the traits and deeds only but with the very identity of the other. The love or hatred of someone is not constituted by the sum of valuings of physical characteristics or traits of personality; rather, it is because these traits are those of the one I love or hate that they become adorable or despicable. For Levinas, parental love is not simply directed to the core identity of the child; in that love the existence of the child is referred back to itself and first acquires its identity.

6. *The Nature of the Libido*

The other is a visible, palpable physical entity, belonging to the same kind as myself. For Sartre, this is a judgment made by a third party whose subjectivity situates both of us in his field of objects; for Merleau-Ponty, it is a recognition first produced by the intercorporeality out of which my own vision forms. The coalescence with the others is the constitutive operation that brings me to nature. Nature, the common field of mundane activities, reservoir of the objects of objective knowledge, is the transcendent correlate of an intercorporeality and the anonymous, universal perception it exercises. The transcendental constitutive subjectivity, Merleau-Ponty says, is intersubjectivity. But by virtue of its intercorporeal basis the community of subjects is included in nature, figuring there as psychophysical agents.

What makes the relationship with the other strangely dramatic is that it also involves a metaphysical breakthrough. For Sartre, the relationship with the other begins with contact with a transcendental constitutive source of the world. This transcendental reality of the other is radically different from the psychophysical phenomenon he is in perceived nature, to the point that it is only when this vanishes that contact with the other's subjectivity is really made. Access to the other as transcendental subjectivity is made through something like a transcendental deduction—a thought that posits the founding instance on the basis of the evidence of the founded. For Sartre, it is not the psychophysical phenomenon the other presents in the physical world that functions as the basis of this deduction. It is one's own sudden inscription in the physical sphere, as a sensible object, that is the evidence for the extraphysical, transcendental reality of the other.

For Levinas the alterity of the other makes contact only in the form of an interruption of the continuity of phenomena, a disturbance of order. The face of another is present as the trace of something that passed without having presented itself and without being re-presentable. There is not a totality of nature whose coherence and cohesion supports the reality of the other; alterity is evident only in the interruptions and disruptions of the phenomenal order, which prevent it from closing in on itself. Metaphysical experiences interrupt the continuity of physical experience.

These occur when the psychophysical phenomena of the other are encountered as points of disruption in the natural order, when with his sensible surfaces the other faces— appeals as a destitution in the fullness of things, contests the order by which the scene and the field are mine. The irreducible alterity of the other is evident not in the significant movements with which gestures may break step with natural rhythms, in the ephemeral words that seem to convey a tangible presence so much in excess of their physical insignificance, but in the appeal and command with which eyes look, voice sounds and dies away, hands handle emptiness. These are the *phenomena* of alterity. They do not have the structure of profiles which make evident a sensible thing in reality, nor of sensible signs designating an ideal identity. They are, Levinas says, *traces* of the passing of alterity.[13]

Eroticism is the experience of the very flesh and substance of another, beneath words and gestures and postures, as traces of alterity. The ultramaterial substance of another obsesses, as a breach of the physical membrane of mundane reality. Its movements and positions divested now of all signifying or expressive intent, of all spirituality, masses now seemingly delivered over to the universal laws of gravity and dynamics, obtrude as loci of pure disruption of nature. This very flesh, exposed and palpable, no longer sighing subtle meanings, heavy and panting, no longer illuminating a field of significance, incandescent with ardor, afflicts the physical and natural continuity, afflicts me and the phenomenal field I appropriate, as other. In the contact of our common flesh, the spasm of disorder that demoralizes my position is a trace of radical alterity. The approach of the other is dismemberment of the natural body, fragmentation of the phenomenal field, derangement of the physical order, breakdown in the universal industry.

For Levinas, erotic receptivity for alterity is located on the periphery, in the most elementary tropisms of sensibility, at the level where life is not yet receptivity for sense data, givens of meaning, but only vibration of enjoyment in a carnal substance. The sensibility is sensual and libidinal inasmuch as it is affected not with a nutritive element to be assimilated, but with a plenitude over and beyond any notion or possibility of assimilation, stricken by the contact with alterity. Levinas distinguishes two tropisms of sensibility: assimilation (sensing is savoring) and susceptibility, capacity to be affected by alterity. In sensuality the tropism of susceptibility that ex-ists, that is stupefied by alterity, is not separate from the tropism of sensibility that turns in an involution of enjoyment. These processes have to be exhibited by a kind of phenomenal analysis, a kind of physics that locates the sensibility within the sensible—and locates the other in the evidence of his traces.

But this kind of analysis requires also that a physics, a phenomenology of nature, be elaborated, in which nature is no longer monadic, no longer a totality everywhere synthesized by laws. It is nature itself that is metaphysical! The most elementary tropisms of sensibility encounter the absolutely inassimilable, the absolutely strange. Such a physics would not develop in the direction of Levinas's own phenomenology of the elements, the earth and the goods of the earth, as sketched out in *Totality and Infinity*. For those fragments of a phenomenology of nature were conceived to articulate nature precisely as the "sphere of the Same," as a totality lived before it is conceptually represented as a totality synthesized scientifically in laws. What could such a physics be, and how could it be elaborated? Only the requirement for it can be found in Levinas's final philosophy.

4.

The Intensive Zone

Levinas takes the phenomenological idea of interpreting the libidinal impulse as intentional to the limit: libidinal existence turns wholly on alterity, and its fecundity is the ultimate form of the movement of ex-istence out of its own state of being. But this intentionality or ex-istence no longer posits, comprehends in advance, an objective; the other to which it is oriented is incomprehensible, inappropriatable. Jean-François Lyotard, following Freud and Nietzsche, suppresses entirely the teleological reference in the libidinal impulse, to conceive of it as a vector of force without any objective, a gratuitous excess, an intensity. With this idea he constructs a quite new image of the libidinal body. It is not only, as in Levinas, contrasted with the expressive organism or the functional, practognostic organism; it is contrasted with the organism structure as such. The orgasmic surface is not an organism. The organism belongs to nature, is determined by the biochemistry, anatomy, and physiology that integrate it into the universal determinisms of material nature. The orgasmic surface deflects the functional operations that connect with the circuits of nature; it extends itself, propounds its inorganization, its intensive circulations, across whatever it comes in contact with. Yet Lyotard does not conceive of the organic and the orgasmic as the phenomenal, the physical, and what is radically other, metaphysical. These overlap, appropriate one another. The organic takes shape in the erotogenic zone of what Freud called the "primary processes"; but the organism itself will function as an orgasmic surface, its very fixations and bound energies giving way to new circulations of intensities.

1. The Erotogenic Surface

In "the most obscure and inaccessible region,"[1] or in the beginning, at the core of life, there are excitations. Of themselves they are intensities, moments of potential that accumulate and discharge, moments of feeling, both pleasure and unpleasure.

They are surface effects. They occur at the point of conjuncture between a hand and a breast, a thigh and another thigh, lips and another's lips, lips and the pulp of fruit, toes and sand. They do not occur on a pregiven surface, but by occurring they mark out a surface, make skin, hair, vulva, exist for themselves and not for the sake of the interior or of the whole. Surface effects, they do not express an inward or deep meaning, or signify an exterior object or objective. They are effects without causes—it is an elementary datum of psychoanalysis that an excitation can be out of all proportion to the stimulus that provoked it.

And they are, Freud said, timeless. "This means in the first place that they are not ordered temporally, that time does not change them in any way and that the idea of time cannot be applied to them."[2] An intensity is not a present as phenomenology understands the term, a presenting process, surpassing but thereby retaining a past of itself, projecting or anticipating a future of itself. It is sheer passing, discharge. It is *a tense*, Lyotard says—a singular tense. A movement, a moment, a passing, without memory and without expectations, ephemeral and useless, which can thus be surprised and be as a surprise—that is, be a pleasure and an unpleasure.

Freud supposed that unpleasure corresponds to an increase in the quantity of the unbound excitations, and pleasure to a diminution. The organism endeavors to keep the quantity of excitation present in it as low as possible or at least to keep it constant. An organism tends to stability, to return to the quiescence of the inorganic world. The universal tendency of all living substance is in reality a death drive. But the organism endeavors to ward off any possible ways of returning to inorganic existence other than those that are immanent in itself. If it endeavors to neutralize every excitation that occurs in it, it does so only in order to be able to pursue the form of death immanent in itself.

But, Lyotard points out, there is also a death drive immanent to the excitation as such, a compulsion of excess potential to discharge itself. "We have all experienced how the
greatest pleasure attainable by us, that of the sexual act,"
Freud wrote, "is associated with a momentary extinction of a
highly intensified excitation."[3] It occurs without regret and
even without recall. The pain involved in the libidinal intensity is that of its own excess, and not simply of a constituted
organism's being overcharged. The excess is positive; it is incompossible figures being affirmed at once; it is multiple, scis-
sioning ways in which the intensity seeks to disintegrate and
discharge. It is the Bacchantes' frenzy with the masks of contradictory goat-gods over the masks of their civic womanhood.
It is the disorder of amorous nonsense mumbling and insisting
open up, take me, don't, tighten hold and release me, come
and stop, obey and command. It is the babbling of pleasure of
the infant holding to the maternal arm with its lips, the stout
shoulder holding the dry infantile thirst, maternal eyes seeking the oscillations of their pleasure in the unfocused infantile
orbits. What Freud characterized as the free mobility of the
primary-process excitations constitutes their intensity. In
psychedelic terms, they are "speed."

The libidinal excitations do not invest a pregiven space;
they extend a libidinal surface. This surface is not the surface
of a depth, the contour enclosing an interior. The excitations
do not function as signals, as sensations. Their free mobility is
horizontal, and continually annexes whatever is tangent to the
libidinal body. On this surface exterior and interior are con-
tinuous; its spatiality that of a Moebius strip. The excitations
extend a continuity of convexities and concavities, probing
fingers, facial contours, and orifices, swelling thighs and
mouths, everywhere glands surfacing, and what was protuber-
ance and tumescence on the last contact can now be fold,
cavity, squeezed breasts, soles of feet forming still another
mouth. Feeling one's way across the outer face of this Moebius
strip one finds oneself on the inner face—all surface still and
not inwardness. The paths of free mobility turn upon themselves without issuing on a source or an exit, describing a
labyrinthine space by their displacement and passage. There
are intersections and encounters, and the encounter is each
time fled in terror or in gaiety, and the flight traces out trans-

parent walls, secret thresholds, open fields and empty skies in which the encounter is eluded, diffused, forgotten. The agitated caressing hand is not seeking an entry, a hold, or a secret; it is only departing from the point of encounter, getting lost, describing a space in which it can lose itself.

An intensification incites intensifications in the entourage. It is not a desire for, an intention aiming at, a lack of these further excitations. They do not complement or complete one another; their constellation does not constitute a totality or a system. Lyotard conceives of their relationship as jealousies. Jealousy is not only a reaction-formation within the Oedipus triangle, expressing penis envy and homosexual identification. It is already in the primary process; it is the way a singular tensor incites other singular impulses without causally transmitting its force or its form to them. The force that intensifies at any point impresses the surrounding forces, pumps off their energy, and tears from the environs exhalations and intensifications. Every intensity induces intensities—jealousy of the vulva for the mouth, jealousy of the nipple for the fondled testicles, jealousy of the woman over the book her lover is writing, jealousy of the sun upon the closed shutters behind which the reader reads that book.

The libidinous labyrinth is extended both by the displacement of the intensity made of the unstable affirmation of incompossible forces, and by the intensifications of jealous sites. The displacement of intensity is both its expansion, describing an extension, arousing jealous intensifications beyond itself, and its dissipation, describing a space without verticality, the essentially supine libidinous zone. If Nietzschean exultation is the feeling of every expanding and elevating power, the incredulous and insolent laughter of libidinous excitement assents to nothing, posits nothing, and awaits no one's recognition, disperses in self-mocking dissolution.

2. The Organism

Life begins in the libidinal incandescences that circulate and describe an erotogenic zone. But it organizes itself into a functional and expressive apparatus—an organism. For Lyotard, the determinative factor in an organism is not the tele-

ological axis that would make the limbs and organs representatives of or substitutes for one another within the whole,
or the intentional arc that would take everything exciting the
organism as a reference toward something absent, something
beyond. That in Lyotard's view is a metaphysical interpretation of the essence of an organism. He instead seizes upon the
Freudian idea that an organism is the locus where the originally freely mobile excitations are bound, that is, fixed, determined, acquire identity and position with respect to one
another. What first makes excitations significant and functional is not their individual reference to absences, objectives
outside the organism, but their distribution relative to one
another within the organic space. Lyotard conceives of the
process as a slowing down of the excitations. Each intensity
was a simultaneous affirmation of incompossible vectors; the
tension of their incompossibility now slackens and the excitation becomes an excitation of *this* rather than *that*. The excitation is maintained in its identity and tends toward a *nonthis*
that is reserved, passed by, or deferred, yet to come. By virtue
of this tension toward what is deferred, temporally removed
from it, the excitation acquires the character of a *trace*. The
inner space of an organism is constituted as this retentional
field, the memory of intensities, localization of their passage.

According to Freud, an organism forms when "an undif-
ferentiated vesicle of a substance that is susceptible to stimulation"[4] forms a protective shield for itself, that is, constitutes
for itself an inwardness. The protective shield is formed by the
outermost surfaces of living substance which cease to have the
structure proper to living matter and become to some degree
inorganic. This deadening of the outer layer of the organism
functions to protect the living vesicle from the lethal force of
energies penetrating from the external world. Its closure
makes of it a theater in which the external world is represented. For the paths of the binding processes in developed
species are sense organs which deal with only very small
quantities of external stimulation and take in only samples, or
representatives, of the external world. The organism is itself a
totality within which parts can substitute for one another, represent one another. It is the theater of an inner political economy.

To conceive of the libido as an organic function or an intentionality, as Merleau-Ponty did, is to try to understand it in terms of the body qua organism, that is, the body organized as a protective system against death by shock by a partial deadening of itself. The functioning of the primary life-force, the libido, according to Lyotard's argument, cannot be derived from this secondary lethal system. The primary and essential life-libidinous forces lie in an erotogenic zone that preceded the constitution of the body as an organism, a zone that has to be described in its own right. Every orgasmic event occurs as a point of breakup in the body as organism, a disintegration and dismembering, a reversion to preorganic erotogenic carnality.

Freud first came upon the death drive as the meaning of systems of repetition-compulsion, whereby even the most painful things return—as in the dreams of traumatic neuroses. These partial systems are fixations that block the circulation of excitations and disrupt the equilibrium of the whole organism. But the whole organism is formed in a fixing and binding of excitations. Freud supposed that the freely mobile excitations are fixed, bound, so that they can be disposed of— neutralized. The organism resists every destruction by shock and by internal disequilibrium, but is itself wholly a process of neutralization of the free mobility of excitations—return to the quiescence of the inorganic. It resists every death that befalls it or invades it, in order to pursue its own paths to the inorganic.

Lyotard criticizes a teleology implicit in the Freudian conception, which makes of death the telos invented in the organism, and the organism the telos of the primary process erotogenic zone. The death drive Freud first found in the systems of repetition-compulsion, as partial systems that function to block the circulation of excitations within the whole organism. Yet the bound configurations that hold excitations, the inhibitions and the neuroses, are also loci where force intensifies. The malfunction produced in the organism as a whole by these partial organisms force excitations to invest in this solidified channel or elude it in devious ways. The fixing of paths and the determining of operations engender the deviations. New itineraries for the discharge of excitations and pleasures, new modalities of the pleasure principle issue from the death drive that takes form in the partial systems, the compulsive and repetitive operations, the stabilized disorders and memory systems. At the point where the structure is fixed, and holds, there arises the levity of an inundation of force breaking through the dam, and the exuberance of detours found; excitement of compounds breaking up upon other compounds and pain of what does not give; impatience surging from this gaiety and this pain that the investments still hold, that the abyss does not draw them violently enough. When on the body of a hysteric segments of the libidinal surface are desensitized, excluded from the circulation of affects, when muscles contract and lock, respiratory channels tighten and become asthmatic, the engirdled and besieged systems begin to function on their own: the contracted muscles, the tightened respiratory system pit their bound forces against resistances like separate organized mechanisms. Psychoanalysis will be able to find in them their own logic, their own system, their own intelligibility. The partial organization is lethal inasmuch as it obstructs and disrupts the larger organism with which it is bound; in it excitations are fixed and the hysteric seized in sterile repetitions. Yet the malfunction produced in the larger organism also intensifies the excitations where they are blocked, so that they invest in this bound system, break against it, or find devious paths of release. The crazed laughter that chokes the asthmatic, the local impotencies that drain off the force of those who shy away from the exercise of force, the obsessions that disintegrate the schizophrenic—as also the panic that dissipates the exuberance of militants in a political demonstration—relieve and release the organism from the lethal system it is. These malfunctions and compulsive disorders ravage the organism, disrupt its immanent and general pursuit of its death, derail it in peripheral excitations and pleasures.

The phenomenological identification of the libido with the intentional arc in the organism was then, for Lyotard, not only mistaken in that it failed to understand that the organism itself forms out of the primary process libidinal zone. It—and psychoanalysis—also mistakenly see the organism as simply functional, as the locus of the reality principle. In fact, the secondary processes which fix the organism, and its internal fixated malfunctions, engender primary processes in turn. The death drive fixed in it forces excitations to become freely mobile anew, that is, it delivers them over to their own death drive. As far as the organism extends the orgasmic surface also extends.

3. Semiotics and Intensive Circulation

The fixing, that is, the deadening of the outer surfaces of the living substance forms for it a protective shield against the invasion of external stimulation, Freud tells us. The paths of the binding processes in developed species are sense organs; they take in, as we have noted, only samples, or representatives, of the external world. In an organism the excitations function as signs, they are "sense data."

In an organism. . . . Lyotard holds up Freud's energetics and psychic economics against phenomenology; he refuses the phenomenologist's assertion that the libidinal surface has to be conceived as a fabric of meanings which is unconscious, that is, dissimulated under and by the expressed meanings. If, as Lacan set forth, the unconscious is structured like a language, that, Lyotard thinks, is not to be taken to mean that its elements are significations. The sensuous excitations of the erotogenic surface are taken as signs inasmuch as they are conceived to contain an intentional reference beyond themselves, a reference to absence. The surface of excitations is made into a field of sensations by being set on the axes of ideal significance, according to Husserl, or upon the world, according to Merleau-Ponty, or upon the phallus of the castrated organism, according to Lacanian psychoanalysis. All these conceptions Lyotard denounces as metaphysical. They understand the organism, and its surfaces, in function of a Beyond. Lyotard seeks to understand it in function of the primary processes which it binds—and which it does not surpass, since all the fixations, all the protective shields which partial and whole organisms extend about themselves, also function as surfaces for the free circulation of excitations.

The organism forms in a fixed distribution of excitations whose reference to one another is, according to Lyotard, their retarded encroachment on one another. Each is what it is, then, in view of the others. As such, they are sensations, and are organized as a semiotic system. It is this positive reference to one another, made of a slow-down movement into one another, and not a reference to absence, ideality, or negativity, that makes them semiotic terms.

This semiotic field is also a surface of libidinous effects. Lyotard refuses to identify these effects with a second system of signs, refuses to make all the manifest signs refer also metaphorically to the phallus. The libidinal effects are intensities, points of compacted excess, and not relay points for meaning. They do not link up by metaphorical reference to ideal or unreal significations, nor by metonymical reference to further signs, but induce "jealous outbursts" in other loci of intensification about themselves. The semiotic movement itself extends the field for libidinal intensifications; the signs are material, and collect as so much material for libidinal conflagration. Certain terms in the sign-system, such as proper nouns, hardly refer to meanings at all, and are not univocally defined in function of the difference they mark from other terms; in them incompossibles can short-circuit and excitations intensify.

Flechsig, for example, for Judge Schreber,[5] is not a term that signifies simply the function of doctor, and as a generic designation it does not designate by itself a singular individual. The term is susceptible to giving rise to incompossible positings; *Flechsig* is doctor, aristocrat, cop, God, the female seducer of Schreber. On the surface of excitations, outer face and inner face are contiguous; *Flechsig* is designated by a locus on Schreber's body, an intensification in the anal zone. The organ ceases to function biologically, as a conduit for the wastes rejected by the whole organism; it is dismembered from the whole to figure as the locus on the libidindal surface where the name *Flechsig* covers a collage of intensive processes. *Flechsig* appears there as the unnatural, cretinous power that prevents Schreber's anus from functioning as an integral part of the organism, prevents Schreber from defecating. The anus no longer knows what it is for and what it conducts; this stupidity is the persecution by the unnatural or supernatural *Flechsig*, a God "[so] blinded by His ignorance of human nature [that He] can positively go to such lengths as to suppose that there can exist a man too stupid to do what every animal can do—too stupid to be able to sh—."[6] Shitting is now possible only by miracle. What Freud called the anaclitic deviation of the organ-function, which produces the libidinous surface-effect, is, in positive terms, the intensification of the anal surface such that it becomes the locus of miracles. The persecution by the divine *Flechsig* is not prohibition and castration only, but, in positive terms, *Flechsig's* craving to fill this anal zone with all his own supraplenary presence, his divine compulsion to sodomize Schreber to all libidinal supratemporality or eternity. In gender incompossibility: *Flechsig*, the divine sodomite, would impregnate the judge.

Here there are not simply *my* paranoid feelings "projected" on a term that functions simply as a signifier. The proper name does not identify an ego but designates an effect occurring at a confluence of multiple excitations (like the "Kelvin effect" in physics); what requires a proper name is excitations that cannot be aligned along common paths or appropriated by an ego.

> The name *Flechsig* takes hold of the most unexpected regions of the libidinal strip, or rather makes them exist as chunks of the vast *anonymous* maniac erectile labyrinth—Ah, you think you are a doctor reducing my solar anus to the wretched proportions of Oedipal pregenital regression! In saying "Flechsig," in building on "Flechsig" my metaphysical and historical novel, in putting "Flechsig" at the beginning and at the end of my hatreds and my loves, I make of you, Doctor, not a pawn in my paranoid game, as you think, but an unforeseeable strip of the immense band where anonymous influxes circulate. "Your" name is the guarantee of anonymity, the guarantee that these impulses belong to no one, that no one, and not even "the doctor" is sheltered from their movements and their investments.[7]

If proper names, with their margin of semantic indeterminacy, can function as loci for intensification on the libidinal surface, so also can the terms most determined by the system of other terms, by alterity, the terms most referential of ideality and negativity.

> We don't even have to say: that big Zero—what crap! After all, it is a figure of desire, and where are we to establish ourselves so as to deny it this quality? In what other no less terrorist Zero? *One cannot establish oneself* on the twisted, electricized seisms of the labyrinthine band. Let us get this into our heads: the instantiation of the intensities on a Nothing that would be the origin, on an Equilibrium, and the folding back of whole parts on the libidinal Moebius strip to form a theatrical volume are the result not of an error, illusion, orneriness, a counterprinciple, but of desire again. The forming into representations is a desire, the putting on a stage, in a cage, in jail, in a factory, in a family,

in a box, is desired. Domination and exclusion are desired. Extreme
intensities are instantiable also in those set-ups. The black Pharaoh
had the death, had the metamorphosis he sought, had been that death
he was.[8]

4. *The Passionate Depersonalization*

Lyotard argues that the libidinous dependency is fraudu-
lently interpreted by Sartre—and by Sade—in dialectical
terms, in terms of mastery and slavery—"all that is so much
virile crap." In Schreber's "fundamental language," *Flechsig*
does not designate univocally a unitary and transcendent
sovereign subject, but the intensive effects evident in Schreber's constipation and diarrhea, in the disconnecting of the organ-function and the hallucinatory investment that accumu-
lates there. In Schreber's anus *Flechsig* becomes supernatural
and divine in his ignorance of human nature and his captiva-
tion by the female allurements of Judge Schreber. To interpret
all that as a masochistic will on the part of Schreber to put
himself under the domination of *Flechsig* is to ignore the fact
that in Schreber's hole the doctor can no longer hold on to his
identity nor God onto His sovereignty. Here nothing is face to
face. Whatever *Flechsig* does or says reverberates in un-
foreseeable ways to torment Schreber's anal zone, and every
discharge, every anal sensation activates the tragic-comic succession of masks answering to the name *Flechsig*.

Orgasm as organic destructuration is certainly an abandon
of the force and implements of the body, but not in view of
being of use in the constitution of the other's organism—or his
incarnate subjectivity. In ex-prostitute Xavière Lafort's explanation:

Punishment is again a way of making a human being accept the inac-
ceptable. But the S-M bond also ends up making you feel something
for your pimps. This "something" is nameless; it is beyond love and
hatred, beyond feelings, a wild joy mixed with shame, the joy of taking
it, enduring the blow, of belonging and of feeling freed of freedom. It
must exist in all women, in all couples, in lesser or unconscious de-
grees. I really can't explain it. It's a drug, like a feeling of living your
life several times at once, in incredible intensity. The pimps themselves in inflicting these punishments experience this "something,"
I'm sure. . . . I am not saying that I want to go back to that life. But you

always do miss it. It's cocaine. You never find such intensity in normal life.[9]

This "feeling something for" one another is here not a matter of polarization into agents that exercise or receive domination; it is not identifiable as a feeling of domination, since the pimps experience the same "something." It is not a matter of a dialectic of affirmation and negation, love or hatred, as it is not a matter of freedom—the freedom that Sartre's masochist exercises in provoking all the initiatives of his torturer. It is the intensity of living an indeterminate number of lives at once. Here there is no maintaining of the identity and selfhood that could sustain power roles, or the consistency that could give one the abject glory of finding oneself objectified. There is abolition of the center, an offering of thighs, open cheeks, anus, outcast limbs, dismemberment of the dissolute body. "In the navel of the night, in the exhaustion of hands and looks, penis and vulva in shreds, scorched earth devastated without any tactic pursued, there can yet arise in the hoarse and intimate throat of a woman this order: Use me."[10] What use is all this scorched earth? What orders here is a longing that the other perish along with the self, that the limits of exclusion be pushed further, the longing for an immense surface of tangency and intensity. It is neither a potlatch act of defiance nor a wily scheme for ensnaring an alien and menacing sovereignty. Use me: put these organs, these glands into connections they were not made for, extend the libidinal strip without overall plan, by patchwork, by bricolage.

For Lyotard, the libidinous relationship is not an intersubjectivity or even an intercorporeality. There is in his understanding no longer a subject of the libido structured as having an identity, issuing acts out of its spontaneity and ascribing them to itself. There is no longer a subjectivity incarnate as an organism. To become passionate is to become an anonymous conductor of a circulation of libidinous effects, a dismembered body over which intensifications undergo their metamorphoses. There is not *a* libido that would be behind all that, and that could be identified with the consciousness or the intentional arc of the organism. An identity, incarnate subjectivity, even an organism—none of these are the telos of the libidinal processes.

"One has to operate on the pricks, the vaginas, the assholes, the skins, so as to make love be the condition for orgasm"—that is what the lover, man or woman, dreams about, in order to escape the frightful duplicity of the surfaces traversed by impulses. But this operation would be an appropriation or, as Derrida says, a propriation, and then a semiotics, in which the erections and discharges would infallibly signal impulsive movements. But there dare not be such an infallibility—that is our ultimate and supreme recourse against the terrors of powers and the true. That fucking not be guaranteed one way or the other, either as a proof of love or as a gauge of indifferent exchangeability, that love, that is, intensity, slip in fortuitously, and that conversely intensities withdraw from the skins of bodies (you didn't come?) and pass over to the skins of words, sounds, colors, kitchen tastes, animal odors and perfumes, that is the dissimulation we will not escape, that is the anguish, and that is what we have to want. But this will is itself something beyond the capabilities of any subjective freedom; we can meet this dissimulation only *laterally, neben,* as blind escapees, since it is unendurable and there is no question of making it lovable.[11]

Where does the erotogenic strip start and where does it stop? Where do organisms start and where do they stop? The intensities of the primary process are excitations at the conjunction of one's own surfaces with one another, of one's surfaces with those of another, of one's surfaces with those of the physical and social world. There is a libidinous economy at work in the very circulation of goods and services that constitutes the political economy of capitalism. The same processes take pleasure in constituting systems and organic totalities that are at work in thought and in the organization of the body politic—the thought that, like that of the young Marx, depends on the idea of society as an organic totality. At every point in his book Lyotard follows the movements of the psyche writ large on the modern capitalist state. If his analyses are more than simple analyses, they are not so much also critical— where criticism would denounce the movements of the capitalist political economy in the name of a more rational, more coherent, and ultimately more organic conception of the whole—as they are excited by certain effects—the May '68 general strike in France, the Berkeley Free Speech movement, the Prague springtime—belonging more to the order of events than of movements, potentials rather than power, intensities rather than actions, belonging to the libidinal rather than to the political economy.

5. Phenomenology and Metapsychology

Lyotard's work can be called phenomenological in the minimal sense that it is a descriptive and not explicative account of the libidinal effects where they occur in fields for which other disciplines can give accounts by taking these effects as physical, physiological, biological, or social realities. Psychoanalytic methods, as well as a certain literature—Augustine, Artaud, Schreber, Klossowski—which does not report on but exhibits unconscious impulses, supply data and a vocabulary for Lyotard's account. For Lyotard, there is no direct and autonomous access to the libidinal sphere through phenomenological self-consciousness. He has not, like Sartre, put all the reality of libido within the sphere of consciousness, and made consciousness that which cannot exist without being transparent to itself. Sexual impulses are not reflexive processes in which an ego-identity is formed and maintained.

Lyotard distinguishes between the semiotic configurations that form in the sphere of the organism—the organism itself is a representational system, a theater—and the patterns of intensities that circulate in them. But the libidinal effects are themselves representational. For phenomenology, the representational operation is not production of "mental images" but disclosure of being itself, in the form of phenomena—objects or objectives. This Lyotard denies. In his view the intensive excitation does not "aim at" an entity in order to disclose it; it is not a verification of the world. These surface effects also do not depend on their own representations functioning as lures. The phantasm produced in libidinal excitations would have to be neither a true apparition of the beings themselves—would have to be false—nor an advance presentation of an objective—would be dissembling rather than divinatory. Lyotard's libidinal economics requires an epistemology of phantasms, and it further requires—an enormously difficult task!—a theory that would explicate the production of true phenomena out of the false phantasms of the primary process—that is, describe the passage from the pleasure principle to the reality principle.

Lyotard's discourse, attempting to reformulate the concepts applicable to libidinal processes in clearer ways, is principally directed against phenomenological intentionalism and also against Lacanian neo-Hegelianism, which understands sexual desire qua desire to be a demand for what is irremediably absent, understands the desire in libido to be inaugurated by castration. Lyotard draws out the consequences of an abandon of phallic and reproductive normality. His rejection of the organism as telos is one of these consequences.

In addition, Lyotard takes the socioeconomic field to possess libidinal reality, and frames his concepts in such a way that they would also function as the principal terms of a kind of post-Marxist political economics. Since Plato, the concepts framed for the body have been employed to conceive of the body politic, and conversely the body has been conceived in terms of legislative and executive concepts. Lyotard wishes to relate this organism-body with that other body, the orgasmic body or libidinal zone, not only in individual but also in social behavior-theory.

Lyotard's formulations are provisional and await the universal theory, metaphysics in the Aristotelian and Whiteheadian sense, a unified categorial system that would function to establish translatability between data accounted for in physical terms, those accounted for in psychic terms, and those accounted for in socioeconomic terms. Lyotard himself would certainly prefer to think of it as a universal materialism which would then be integrated into the other regional disciplines.

5.

The Carnal Machinery

The new metapsychology, the universal materialist theory integrating psychic phenomena with social, political, economic, technical, and physical phenomena is boldly plotted out by Gilles Deleuze and Félix Guattari in the two volumes of their *Capitalism and Schizophrenia, Anti-Oedipus* and *Thousand Plateaux*. They call it schizoanalysis.

1. *Molar and Molecular*

The first book pursues an unremitting polemic against psychoanalysis and against the Oedipus triangle within which psychoanalysis conducts its analyses and elaborates its theory of the libido. Psychoanalysis takes sexual desire to be polarized by persons, the personages of the authoritative-idealizing father, the enveloping-nourishing mother, and the always premature child who is always ahead of his forces. Libidinal investment in more vast biological and social arenas would occur only through desexualization and sublimation.

Michel Foucault elaborated a momentous new explanation of how the psychoanalytic ideology had become possible. His *Madness and Civilization* presented a vast semi-Marxist, semi-Nietzschean exposition of, first, power structures since the end of the Middle Ages through which the social field of reason and unreason was circumscribed; second, the imagery that arose in this field; third, the moral and medical practices that this imagination commanded; and, last, the ideology that consolidated that praxis. With the decoding of earth and despot and state by the disintegrating effects of capitalism, madness is no longer lived as alienation from the earth and the cosmos or from the body of the despot; it is lived and recognized as alienation from the law of reason. Yet at the very time when modern social and economic developments were progressively reducing the family as a unit of production and social integration, the family came to be invested as the last bastion where reason is authority and law oppression. The modern asylum for the unsocialized was set up, after the French Revolution in France and simultaneously by Quaker reformers in England, not as a medical institution but as a *home*. The doctor figured there not as a professional dispenser of scientific information but as a figure of law and of the authority of reason, an essentially paternal authority in an enclave of juridic minors. It was as such that he worked whatever effects he worked on the behavior of the inmates. The modern psychoanalyst, abandoning the crypto-medications with which the pretense of practicing something analogous to organic medicine had been maintained, inherits the moral and family prestige of the asylum doctor, acts and thinks out of this prestige.

The theory of the Oedipus complex could then be formulated to identify the essence of madness as alienation from the nuclear social institution, the patriarchal family. The psychoanalytic disalienation is to take the same path as the alienation; if madness is "the dull thud of instincts hammering at the solidity of the family as an institution and at its most archaic symbols," "the unending attempt to murder the father,"[1] the treatment consists in finally achieving reconciliation through transference of the conflict upon the personage of the doctor, and the cure consists in the patient being made capable of assuming fully the father or mother persona, founding an Oedipal family in turn. Deleuze and Guattari comment: "Instead of participating in an understanding that will bring about genuine liberation, psychoanalysis is taking part in the work of bourgeois repression at its most far-reaching level."[2]

For Deleuze and Guattari the "first evidence" is that sexual desire does not have as its objects persons or things at all. It is invested in whole environments, in vibrations and fluxes of all kinds; it is essentially nomadic. It is always with worlds that we make love.[3] "Sexuality is everywhere, in the way a bureaucrat fondles his files, a judge metes out justice, a businessman

makes the money flow, the way the bourgeoisie fucks the pro-
letariat."[4] It is through a reduction and isolation that the libido
is fixed on persons or objects; the objectification is produced
in the constitution of a subject, or a preconsciousness. But
these persons or objects are nexuses of disjunction and conjunction in the biological, social, and historical fields which
have already been invested libidinally and unconsciously.

For psychoanalysis, sexuality in the woman is the female
as lack with regard to a male, lack of a phallus. And a man,
whose impulses are constituted as desire in the castration
complex, is also structured as male with respect to the phallus, which is not his physical penis as perceived or touched,
but the lacking organ he sees desired in the other's eyes. With
the concept of the absent and lacking phallus which is said to
transform impulses into sexual desire, we are dealing with
signifiers and signification, and we are interpreting. The
analysis Deleuze and Guattari practice must suspend this her-
meneutics and catch sight of the libidinal processes in their
formation and their functioning. The molar structures—
organisms and environments—whose functioning is exhibited
in statistical laws, are not formed in operations of the same
kind as those with which they function. They can have a
sense, a goal, an intention. But the molecular elements forming the molar structures *are* formed with the same processes
with which they function; they do not represent, signify, aim
at, or mean anything. Their analysis will not be intentional or
hermeneutical, but functional, a mechanic's analysis.

This mechanic's analysis, which must say how the molecular processes—productions or "machines"—are formed and
how they work is not committed to mechanism, although it
opposes vitalism. By a mechanism we understand a system
that functions according to preestablished connections and
following the order of its component pieces, a system that
does not produce or assemble itself. By a living organism we
understand a system with a synthetic individual and generic
unity that forms and reproduces itself. *Mechanism* is the metaphysical endeavor to explain the individual and generic unity
of living organisms as an effect of mechanical systems; *vitalism* is the endeavor to explain mechanical systems as means
assembled by the synthetic operations characteristic of vital
systems. The universal materialism, the *machinism* of De-

leuze and Guattari negates the explanatory value of the two concepts of unity; a living organism which appears as a single unit is, under the mechanic's analysis, seen to be in fact an enormous number of molecular processes, each of which consists in the formation of a connection—an energy flow—and its interruption and consumption. Deleuze and Guattari name them "desire-machines." The nutritive molecules, the air, the terrestrial base, the implements and apparatuses set up with which the molecular processes of a living organism are connected are not ultimately of different nature. "The lower animals keep all their limbs at home in their bodies, but many of man's are loose, and lie about detached, now here and now there, in various parts of the world."[5] These detached systems with their order, rule and necessity, are coded by the living organism that connects with them; a bumblebee is part of the reproductive system of the clover.

The molar wholes Deleuze and Guattari take to be assemblages known by statistical laws, and not synthetic totalities known by some phenomenological insight into essences. If it is always with worlds that we make love, these vast molar wholes are not synthesized by a self-unifying agency, by the ego as self-identifying identity. Gestaltism in molar structures and the self-synthesizing subjectivity which phenomenology took to correspond to the molar structures of experience are both refused, following a Nietzschean inspiration. We are accustomed to look at ourselves as forming a whole, realizing an individual who bears a proper name; we look upon our members and parts and over our motor phases and think that their combination forms an individual produced out of a unitary center. In reality this is but the illusion of the dominant will in a chaos of forces in conflict. It is by grammatical fiction that one assembles and levels to the same the I that says I think, and that which says I will, and I am sleeping, and I am hoping, and I am dreaming. The center is nomadic and ephemeral; it is often but a stroboscopic effect. There are then not inherent synthesizing essences, but selective processes (which are themselves not finalities at work, but zigzag constructions formed by conjunctures and overlappings by chance) that form molar wholes, in the midst of auto-formative molecular functionings.

2. The Molecular Desire-Machines

The molecular processes, these desire-machines, function and form themselves at once, are productive and reproductive of production. Conceived with this Marxist concept of production, they are envisaged at the juncture of nature and culture; they are not transmuted into processes of negativity, desire that empties itself out to oppose itself to all positive reality or that posits an irremediable phallic absence beyond all satisfaction. The molecular processes produce connections, couplings. They interrupt, disconnect, disjoin flows. They produce satisfaction, pleasure-unpleasure, intensity—a consumption that is consummation. Deleuze and Guattari formulate these operations as three Kantian "syntheses."

The mechanic's analysis of how they work is guided by concepts Deleuze and Guattari have taken from molecular biology, from child psychoanalysis, from schizophrenic literature, and from a Nietzschean reading of our social history. From these disparate discourses they have sought accounts of how the molecular processes of desire take shape and work.

They draw on the research of Jacques Monod, at the point of juncture of microphysics and microbiology. The DNA molecule is the point where, Monod wrote, "randomness [is] caught on the wing, preserved, reproduced by the machinery of invariance and thus converted into order, rule, necessity"[6]—the point at which a functioning is formed, a desire is produced and produces. There is a production of flows, of determinate circulations of energy and their interruption, a selecting, detaching, and remaindering operation, and a forming of transverse connections, inclusive disjunctions, and polyvocal conjunctions. Molecular biology sees here a machine ("with the globular protein we already have, at the molecular level, a veritable machine . . ."[7]), a functioning emerging out of a play of chemical combinations, whose constituent elements and affinities are indifferent and random. The random character of the chemical signals, the indifference to the substrate, the indirect nature of the interactions which the emergent molecule engineers, characterize its functioning and its formation.

This Deleuze and Guattari take as a model for the formation

of libidinal impulses. For infantile sexuality first appears in a
dismembered body as the formation of what Melanie Klein
called part-objects and partial organs. The extraordinary liter-
ary power of the text Deleuze devoted to her works *The
Psycho-Analysis of Children* and *Contributions to Psychoanalysis* in his *Logique du sens*[8] bears witness to the powerful
impression her work had on him and designates that work as
the place where his own key terms were first formed.

    Anti-Oedipus also draws on literary texts by Artaud, Beck-
ett, and Schreber, a body of material taken as fully positive, as
lucid accounts of intensely libidinal existences, schizophrenic
to be sure, incompetent in our social order and interred by it,
accounts written by artists who are prophets of a possible and
possibly emerging social order.

    For schizoanalysis incorporates an analysis of social his-
tory in which the Nietzschean concept of savages and nomads
is taken as defining the infantile stage of our history. A barbarian or imperial stage followed, which in turn issued in our
civilized or capitalist stage, whose final development, in the
full affirmation of capital as a universal decoding and deterritorialization, issues in something like a return to savagery or
schizophrenia. That is how the Maoist kind of French Marx-
ism involved here understands, libidinally, the withering
away of the state. Thus schizophrenization is also a process
that the authors find writ large in our whole social world; it is
the form in which we "make love with the world." The schizophrenic literature of Buchner, Beckett, and Artaud reveals an
experience in which neither man nor nature is a distinct entity, for which there are only processes of production and couplings. Man no longer figures as lord of creation, but as ceaselessly connecting an organ-machine with an energy-machine,
a tree with his body, a breast with his mouth, a sun with his
anus, the eternal custodian of the machines of the universe.[9]

3. Couplings, and the Body without Organs

    Under schizoanalysis, nature, industry, humans, all break
up into productive processes—those of production, distribution, and consumption. These are not distinct and successive;
a process produces production, distributes itself on a record-

ing surface which it produces, and consumes itself, producing voluptuousness, anxieties, and pains. The recording is immediately consumed, and the consummation reproduces production.

Production of production forms desire-machines. There is an emission of a flux, an organ that cuts into it and draws off the flux—breast and mouth, part-object and schiz-organ. Flow of bile, of feces, of urine, of nasal mucus, of sperm, of menstrual blood, of spittle, warbling and simean chatter, flow of light, streams of chromatic substance—desire flows. There is a coupling of a source-machine and an organ-machine. A machine to interrupt, skim off, cut into the flux, produce chunks. The draughts of milk drawn off by the mouth flow, bowels move; this organ-machine is in turn coupled with the urethral canal and anal sphincter that interrupts and releases the flow. These binary couplings extend indefinitely; they have the syntactic-logical form of the "and . . . and then . . ." connective synthesis.

The couplings form and prolong themselves in further couplings. The emission of a flow produces the part-organ that interrupts it and draws it off, and produces a flow in turn, which couples with an interrupting organ. But everything stops, too, for a moment. A stasis is produced, which Deleuze and Guattari, following Artaud, call the "body without organs." The infantile substance, full of flows of milk, blood and feces, sated, now immobilizes, mouth closed, anus tight, eyes shut, receptors plugged, turning to the outside an opaque and impervious skin, curled up in a sphere. The water flows, the feet break into the current, the hands cut into the liquid—then the eyes close, the feelers, torpid, feel nothing; the body catatonic in the tub. Judge Schreber "lived for a long time without a stomach, without intestines, almost without lungs, with a torn esophagus, without a bladder, and with shattered ribs; he used sometimes to swallow part of his own larynx with his food."[10] The plenum produced repels all the couplings. It is not produced as an integration or fusion of them but forms alongside of them like yet another, massive, part. The production of this state of sterility and unproductivity, unconsumable and unreproducing, is the death instinct.

There is cannibalistic aggression against the maternal breast in infantile sucking, aggression against the coupling; in infantile anality there is aggression against the chunks of the alimentary flow fragmented in the digestive canals, revulsion against these noxious substances. The formation-functioning of the anorganic plenum is the original paranoiac machine. The primary repression formative of the unconscious is the repulsion that forms a body without organs. Deleuze and Guattari thus determine the unconscious as a state or position of the body.

But this closed sphere, which the molecular desire-machines irritate, persecute, also forms the surface they mark. It attracts the productions of desire; they adhere to it, are recorded on it. They are not integrated into it; on its closed smoothness they drift, collide, pile up. The surface effects produced on the libidinous plenum are these mirages and prodigies. On the passive, female body of Judge Schreber penetrated by and filled with the divine phallus, the inoperative, disconnected anus, excited by this improductive plenitude, suddenly begins to function again, as though by miracle. It is energized by flows of solar rays and divine sperm, agitations captured elsewhere, in other part-organ couplings that now collide with it. Deleuze and Guattari call the anorganic body, as surface of distribution of the productions of desire, the miracle-machine. Attached to the body without organs, the part-organs and freely mobile fragmented pulses they produce get linked up with one another, in association by passive synthesis. But they are distinct and independent of one another, a pure dispersion, an anarchic multiplicity; they do not fit themselves together into a coherent and consistent discourse. Linkages form by shifts in the distribution, collisions, contractions of distance. The distribution of excitations on the erotogenic surface of the body without organs constitutes a fluid and delirious code, where permutations begin anywhere and develop in any direction. The linkages formed are independent of one another, a pure multiplicity. The relationships are not connective, nor do they emanate from an originative principle that systematically fixes terms in their identity and opposition to one another. So far as the body without organs is concerned, any excitation irritating it is equivalent to any other. They are juxtaposed on it in relationships of disjunctive synthesis, "this . . . or that. . . ." The disjunction does not fix an alternative by fixing two impermutable terms between which a choice would be imposed; here the distribution is "randomness caught on the wing."

In the libidinal body writ large, the *socius*—the body of the earth in the savage or nomadic age, the body of the despot in the barbarian or imperial age, capital in the civilized epoch— is a body without organs. These social structures form spheres of antiproduction closed against the molecular productive processes, but they also form recording surfaces on which the molecular productive processes are inscribed and on which they form delirious and fetishist surface effects. Capital forms not only the register on which the productive processes are recorded but also a medium where they enter into lateral connections, where surplus value is produced, which then activates the pure multiplicity of disparate productive processes in turn, as though by miracle.

4. Voluptuous Subjectivity

Consumption is a third process involved in production; production produces consumption, and consumption is itself a production. It produces subjectivity. Deleuze and Guattari take the subjectivity involved in libidinous existence to be a peripheral and surface effect, a moment of consumption, and not a unitary, deep, constitutive source.

There is repulsion of the part-organs by which the body without organs forms and functions as a paranoiac machine. The closed anorganic body also attracts the processes productive of desire, is marked by them, and, by being the passive surface on which they associate, energizes them in new ways without any initiative of its own—a miracle-machine. The state of tension between the paranoiac machine and the miracle-machine is not simply one of formal or logical opposition, and it is not resolved in the dialectical production of a form which would be stable, a state of zero tension. The tension between the two states, paranoiac machine and miracle-machine, gives rise to new processes with their own code and their own product—a new machine. With a term taken from Michel Carrouges,[11] Deleuze and Guattari name it the celibate machine. For the elements of the paranoiac machine (the irritations, incitements, demands, provocations) and of the mira-

cle-machine (the surface effects, the incandescences, phantasms) are not used to fuel a reproductive machinery; they do
not code the reproductive operations of the genital apparatus.
They are consumed voluptuously. The consumptive process—
an intensive force separated, isolated, absorbed, turning on
itself—is subjectness, a state subjected to itself, subjectivity.
And this consummation is also productive; it produces hal-
lucinations and delirium, visionary states and comprehensive,
comprehending states.

Deleuze and Guattari here elaborate quite the reverse of the
phenomenological idea of incarnate subjectivity. Their celibate machine is not identical with the soul understood as the
integrating form of the body, nor the organism-structure, nor
the body-image producing and produced by the body become
corps propre. All those conceptions would derive from the
relationship between parts and whole in a practical system,
from the body as technical machine and not as a desiring
machinery. They take the body as an apparatus coded, or self-
coding, to do, as Goldstein says, but one thing at a time.[12] The
unitary character of the operation would reveal an identity
from which the parts derive, a distributive principle, an identity which the parts compose, or a totalizing process
elaborated in the differentiation and opposition of the parts.
The celibate machine of Deleuze and Guattari that conjoins
paranoiac machine and miracle-machine is produced as a remainder alongside of them. Torments of pleasure separate and
turn on themselves, engendering spirals of ipseity. Pulses of
pleasure, spasms of pain vibrate on themselves, feel themselves. The eddy of a self is formed in this conjunctive synthesis—multiple, vagabond ipseities, here today, gone tomorrow,
circulating on the surface of the body without organs. These
intensive events do not represent the climax of the whole system or the culminating moment of the system become a whole;
they are points at which a surplus, a residue, is consumed.
Subjectivity on the surface of the closed anorganic body is
"celibate miseries and glories pushed to the limit, clamor sus-
pended between life and death, feelings of intense passage,
pure and raw states of intensity destitute of figure or form."[13]

The subjective states are productive in their turn. They are
visionary, comprehensive. They couple with processes bear-

ing the most remote codes. Nietzsche, in a high-noon ecstasy, identifies with all the names of history, lived through a circle of intensive states in which a form of subjectivity is each time born and consumed without anticipation or regret, on the surface of a circle without fixed center, without central ego: the celibate machine of eternal return.

5. Schizo-eschatology

Such is the machinery of a "man producing himself as someone free, irresponsible, solitary, and joyous, finally able to say and do something simple in his own name, without asking permission, a desire lacking nothing, a flux that overcomes barriers and codes, a name that no longer designates any ego whatever. He has simply ceased being afraid of going mad."[14] *Ceased being afraid of going mad?*—have we not constructed but a theoretical transcription of the last delirious letter Nietzsche wrote while sinking into the final collapse?[15] Is not this ephemeral fulguration of Nietzschean subjectivity, turning under all the names of history, the final dissipation into the night of madness? Is this the moment of breakthrough or of breakdown?

Without doubt, both. To be sure, one cannot live this schizophrenic euphoria; that is, one cannot live it in society. One can take one's place in society only by becoming a seat of responsibility, a singular ego that answers for all the operations that occur in it, turning one's erotogenic body into an organism, a technical machine coded with a universal code, turning a productive and auto-productive source into a system of needs, needs for those things of which precisely society is the depository.

Repression is the conversion of the erotogenic body into such a technical machine. According to psychoanalysis, the instance of law and of absence are incarnate in the father, authority figure and ego ideal. The structuring of the polymorphously perverse and auto-productive body of desire into a technical organism that has interiorized an instance of law, of univocal and social coding, is the work of the Oedipus complex. But if the Oedipal family is a machine for the production of repression, it is also an institution comprehensible in terms of the social oppression it serves.

Society oppressive of the primary libidinous production functions as a codifying machine. It is a megamachine functioning to codify the self-coding of desire-machines with a univocal code that would couple them up linearly with an inexhaustible and individual plenitude, an immense and common body without organs.

The first oppressive coding takes the form of a territorialization. The earth is set up as the socius, a body without organs, which simultaneously repels the desiring machinery of libidinal beings and attracts them, imposes on them a code by the way it attracts them and distributes them over itself, and sets them into production again with this code. Masks, fetishes, talismans, tabooed and enchanted objects, shrines, and sanctuaries function to fix the terms of the social coding. Nietzsche, in the second essay of the *Genealogy of Morals,* first forced our noses into the spectacle of the frightful mnemonics by which the human herd gave itself a memory, a common repository of univocal signs. The coding is a work of circumcising, clitoridectomizing, cicatrizing, tattooing, branding, mutilating the flesh of these animals so resistant to socialization, so as to imprint a memory of signs on them. But it also has to be emphasized that this coding and territorialization was entirely a production of desire. Although Deleuze and Guattari often present it as haunted by the anxiety which the phantom of decoded fluxes of desire evokes and has always evoked, depicting capitalism as the specter which all the prior forms of socius megamachines were set up to conjure, the schizophrenic breakdown as the deluge which the Oedipus complex was set up to dike—this finalist explanation does not carry their conviction. In reality, every oppression is a production, producing its own dividends of tormented exhilaration.

The despot, in the barbarian or imperial epoch, sets himself up as a paranoiac machine that transcends, oversees, and judges the earth and the life attached to it. He appropriates to himself the fertility of the soil, the sun, and the rain, closes all upon himself as a body without organs, makes himself a miracle-megamachine. He overdetermines with imperial codes the original territorialization of nomadic multiplicities.

Capitalism is the civilized megamachine, in which capital

is the universal body without organs, a recording surface in which all the movements of desire are inscribed and marked in the code of the abstract axiomatics of money. It brings about also a decoding of the savage and the barbarian, the territorial and the imperial codes. This megamachine is the most universal and abstract oppression of savage and barbarian libidinous productions, and productive of its own dividends, its fetishes and its pleasures, its private property, and its possessor-consumer points of subjectivity. The Oedipal triangulation is set up as an instrument of codification, of oppression; and for the recalcitrant, the psychoanalytic couch is set aside as the territory in which the Oedipal triangulation is to be assumed and reproduced.

The psychoanalytic institution is not the only machine the capitalist megamachine invents in its unremitting work of recoding all desire on the abstract body of capital; there are also bureaucracies and police, all the artificial and residual, imaginary and symbolic territories—states, regions, family lineage, spiritual fatherlands. But, decoding the earth, decoding the tellurian family, earth-mother and sky-father, and decoding the body of the despot, the authority of blood and the law of lineage, decoding despotism and imperial territorialization, capitalism produces universal proletarians—orphans, stateless ones, nomads, perverts, schizophrenics. And orphan, stateless, nomad, pervert, schizoid pleasures.

> The pervert is one who takes the artifice seriously and plays the game to the hilt; if you want them, you can have them—territorialities infinitely more artificial than the ones society offers us, totally artificial new families, secret lunar societies. As for the schizo, migrating continually, wandering, stumbling about, he pushes ever further into deterritorialization, carrying about the unending decomposition of the socius on his own body without organs. And perhaps those schizo peregrinations are his own way of rediscovering the earth. The schizophrenic stands on the limit of capitalism; he is its inherent tendency brought to fulfillment, its surplus product, its proletariat, and its exterminating angel.[16]

Deleuze and Guattari are not pointing to the schizophrenia produced as the modern form of alienation in order to restate the classical Marxist form of the critique of capitalism in the name of some humanist concept of essence alienated. The schizophrenia of capitalist high culture is not the result of an essential humanity in its artists agonizing in the capitalist decodification of earth, skies, homelands, bloodlines, empires, persons. Artists are prophets and first-born, living experiments of the schizophrenic form of libidinal machinery to be produced.

But does not artistic production cease in the asylum? Can the schizophrenic breakthrough not be at once a breakdown in every case? It would be necessary to produce a society—or rather a withering away of the state and an anarchy, a revolutionary machinery—that would liberate each from the megamachine, the socius. That would leave the body without organs of each as the residue of deterritorialization and desocialization, upon which the desire machinery exciting it and activated by it would elaborate each time and for itself polyvocal and singular codes of desire. The art of the twentieth century—Cézanne, Artaud, Strindberg, Joyce, Beckett—gives an idea of what that will mean. However, from the beginning up to the present, the libidinal machinery of each has turned to produce and to desire its own repression. High culture is a work of cruelty, Nietzsche said; its forces have been nothing but paranoiac machines of oppression. How then could such a revolutionary machinery be produced, and what would it be? Could it have the form of a high culture? Or would it not be an atomistic infantilism? What science, what geometry, could be elaborated by a productive process destructured of its Oedipal triangulation? Could the intensities cover themselves with the names of pagan divinities? Could it build temples to hallow its desires? Could it contract sublime forms? Could there be any up or down?

6.

Libido and Alterity

1. The Libidinal Body

Spirit in Homer is the breath the dying hero releases to the winds; it is not the substantial support of all mental and volitional acts and states. Homeric heros have limbs, organs, fluids; it would not occur to Homer to say that they "had" bodies. The word body *(sōma)* was introduced, Plato says in the *Cratylus,* by the Orphic priests. They said that man was a spirit held captive in the body as in a dungeon *(sēma)*; our incarnation is incarceration. The body was determined with the concept of matter, which in Aristotelian physics is fixed by opposition to the concept of form, and with the concept of mechanism in the epoch of Descartes and Newton.

The contemporary philosophy of libido provokes an upheaval in the concept of body. What is the body if it can be the object of erotic craving? One does not, Sartre remarks, desire anatomy, a corpse or a madwoman. The genital organs are not of themselves erotic. All beauty, Freud wrote, owes its allurement to its latent erotic content, but the genital apparatus, for which beauty is its dissimulation or metaphor, is never beautiful.

For Sartre, the carnal is the presence of subjectivity captured, contained. Its bewitchment is that of the magical, which, in his first philosophical essay on emotions, Sartre defined as a subjective spontaneity degraded, trailing among determinist things. The very idea of capture suggests that the presence of subjectivity in objectivity is forced, not forming a compound, a synthetic whole, a new essence. The pleasure of fondling, caressing, exposing, and penetrating is vindictive, is

103

the triumphant satisfaction of having vanquished the pure and ungraspable threat that another's subjectivity first was. The pleasure is fed with the memory of the danger known, the enslavement undergone. Yet this pleasure is also insecure: the subjectivity of another is not really smelted down in this being, and the nausea Roquentin felt before the root of the chestnut tree, when its significance and all names drifted off from it, the lover also knows over the flesh he seeks to penetrate and possess. Copulation, directing attention to the genital apparatus, organs to be manipulated, orifices to be penetrated, dissipates the erotic perception and gives place to a practical, instrumental relief of the body.

The carnal is essentially suggestive, a veil rather than a profile or side of a sensible thing—or is the profile or side *as a* veil. The look hides the eyes, Sartre wrote; in the carnal the eyes hide again the look, the flesh congeals over the feeling, the judgment is blotted out in the palpability of hands dragged over one. Carnal charm is the effectiveness of the denuded substance of the body to conceal all the subjective powers. What fascinates in the carnal is the sense that in the most palpable organ the most elusive power lurks, in the solidity of substance the most nihilating menace has taken cover. Subjectivity *haunts* space; it is nowhere localizable, and most evident in the distances. Positing the other in the here-and-now of a palpable body makes his subjectivity most absent there, everywhere absent. In the carnal subjectivity is nowhere potency, nowhere implicit, nowhere conceivable, but all artifice, deception, delusion. The carnal is the charm of non-frankness. It does not consist in any objective forms that would have a vocative or imperative force, in any movements that would be organized by a teleological force, in any glands or tissue that would harbor spirituality.

For both Merleau-Ponty and Levinas, phenomenology has to yield an elucidation of the carnal according to its specific phenomenal traits, and not decompose it into subjectivity and objectivity. Throughout his work Merleau-Ponty rejected all thinking-by-composition—being and nothingness are, he wrote, twin abstractions. All his phenomenology is anti-Kantian in that everywhere he refused the analysis into matter and form. One cannot separate even conceptually the significance from the *hylē*, the grain or opacity in a sensible

phenomenon. There is no contour disengaging a figure from
the ground without a significance, a reference to far-off elements; it is the significance that delineates the contour. Sense
perception is the perception of sense, meaning, in material
concreteness. Even with the most elementary sense datum
imaginable, a spot of blue or green, if the opaqueness becomes
perceptible as a spot and as blue or green, it incarnates a sense
of repose and release, which establishes the spot as a
significant contrast and therefore as a spot. Sense qua meaning
and sense qua direction or form are twin abstractions, lifted
from the original configuration, the "world-ray," and do not
really decompose it—as they cannot recompose it. The ultimate terms are relief, contrast, distance, differentiation, grada-
tion, openness; they cannot be compounded out of being and
nothingness.

The carnal appears as particular postures, certain gestures—it is not the haunting invisibility of freedom and judgment. Attitude and position are twin abstractions lifted from
the concrete plenitude of posture; expression and movement
twin abstractions lifted from gesture. Specific to the erotic
configuration of the carnal is that its forms and axes are not
addressed to the outlying implements of the practical field,
but are immediately addressed to one's own body. The agile,
motile body and not the prone or sleeping body is erotically
seductive, because it excites diagrams of apprehension and
taking in the one who witnesses it.

Yet Merleau-Ponty did not attend to what is provocative
and shameless in the erotic exposure. Levinas centers his
analysis of the carnal on this. Provocative, over and beyond
evocative, the carnal is the equivocal and disordered demand
of one denuded and destitute, vulnerable, but also throwing
itself forth, ultramaterial. This excess, this exhibitionism in-
flicts itself on its witness, more pressing still than the frank
facing that is imperative. The erotic gestures do not simply
call for their complements, like the positions of a dancer before his partner; they denude a hopeless mortality before the
complacent compassion of tenderness. The erotic position
does not simply order the looks and the moves of its witness; it
makes extravagant and equivocal demands on his or her substance, afflicting it with a destiny beyond any ordered direction. What Sartre has not seen is that the servitude this denud-

ing appeals for is not existence as an object delivered over to the usages of the other, but tenderness, the complacency of a compassion that goes to join this vulnerability and does not aim to heal. Carnal arousal is devirilization, divestment of body armor. What Sartre has not seen is that what the brazen exhibitionism of the carnal imposes imperatively is not the guilty consent to being an object in its hands—with the ruse such a consent to one's objectification, Sartre has seen, involves. The erotic subjugation is a complicity in view of nothing, an ordinance that has no projects.

And Levinas has shifted the sense of the erotic—the provocative, obsessive, rather than the vocative, imperative, and indicative sense—from the form to the very materiality of the other. What is erotically troubling is not so much positions and movements of a certain style, as the carnal vulnerability and exhibitionist ultramateriality. The carnal is not so much the patterns of the caresses and holds as the susceptibility that afflicts, that pains, that induces tenderness in the agent-organization of its witness. It is not so much diagrams that project order, as proximity, contiguity, tangency, which obsess. For Levinas, what exhibits the carnal is not so much its sense as its excess or equivocation of sense; the denuding of the carnal is profanation from which one discovers nothing, in which nothing is communicated. The carnal is the vulnerability and mortality of flesh that solicits care, the shameless ultramateriality that does not preserve the minimal distances an object needs in order to be present.

Lyotard diagrams the noneuclidean spatiality of the erotogenic zone. It is all surface, a Moebius strip. It is opposed to the closure, and the inner theater, of the organism. The erotic excitations are not sensations, diaphanous matter through which life's intentionality envisages the contours of outside objects. The erotic figure of the other, to which one is libidinously drawn, is also all surface, a surface become contiguous with one's own. The flesh of another does not excite libidinally because of a specific organization or sense; what is essential is that one is oneself excited, that excitations extend a surface in oneself. There is no natural and specific privilege to the genital zone, not even to a body of the same species as oneself, not even to a living body; the surface of erotogenic excitation extends to the surfaces of grass, sunlight, the surface qualities of conversation, music, ideologies, such as that of the young and effeminate Marx. The idea that it was certain proportions of torso and limbs, a certain way of reposing and certain figures diagrammed in motion that were alluring, seductive, feminine, Lyotard puts down to the codes of the time; our tastes are now postclassical and postmodern, we find raucous cries in the female throat as alluring as the airy murmurs, we find the angular and chaotic thrusts as exciting as the patterns of minuets and waltzes. We find them so because they intensify before and break through those organisms. Veils, artifices, deceits, and conceits belong to the proper art of the erotic—but not because the erotic charge lies entirely in the impalpable element of subjectivity, the transcendent that they cover over and betray. Rather, the sphere of the erotic is the Dionysian and Nietzschean ceremony, where the masks only cover other masks, where the very flesh unveiled consists of ever more veils—more surface effects. The glitter of phenomenality without noumenality, of veils and screen behind which there is nothing to be seen, becomes an erotic universe when one is captivated by the pure appearances, forgets the depths or the foundations. The erotic profanes, with a vandalism that prizes only the veils of the tabernacle, that comes to think there is nothing behind the veils.

Deleuze and Guattari agree. For them the erotic is not the tabernacle in which the genital orifices conceal the germs of life's reproduction, but the whole surfaces of worlds. It is from the first with whole worlds that we make love. However, these vast molar wholes are erotic not through their synthetic organization but, in dissolution and dismembering, through the pure multiplicity of molecular processes spread across them. In nomadic times, it was the surface of the earth that formed the anorganic body upon which the couplings of desire were distributed; in imperial times it was the body of the despot; in civilized times it is the abstract body of capital. Each time it is the possibility of couplings, of flows, of interruptions, of the surplus production of a remainder to be consumed, that is the reality of desire, libido, life. The production of the anorganic body makes possible the desire-machines as surface effects.

Lyotard and Deleuze-Guattari certainly refuse every strategy in phenomenology that sets up subjectivity as the constitutive source of structure and meaning. And yet their account of the erotic visage of things—erotogenic surface, desire-couplings, and anorganic body—lacks all that charge of provocation and shamelessness in which Levinas saw the essence of the carnal. It is true that for Levinas the carnal properly speaking is something that happens to the body of another, the body of one that faces. For Lyotard and Deleuze-Guattari the condensation of the carnal on the other is the result of Oedipal repression. But since the carnal for them does not appear through vulnerability and provocation, it is one's own state of excitability alone that determines what surfaces of things and of worlds will be annexed to the libidinal economy.

Merleau-Ponty's exposition of the libidinal body depended on the concept of the organism—a sensory-motor system structured according to postural axes, active in the formation of diagrams of movement. Erotic movements are actions, and are seated in the corporeal practognosis. The erotic sensibility is generalized throughout all the faculties; it is coextensive with the body's sensibility and communicates across the schemata of the body's motility. For Merleau-Ponty, then, the erotic organization of the body is a specification of its reality as an organism.

Lyotard and Deleuze-Guattari have understood the orgasmic body in opposition to the organism. For Lyotard the erotogenic surface extends its eddies over the fixed paths of the organism-structure; for Deleuze and Guattari the surface couplings slide over the anorganic body. For Deleuze and Guattari the organism, system of fixed or bound excitations, tends to closure, inertia, torpor, and the inorganic state.

This inner movement of the organism is missing in Merleau-Ponty. For him the organism is not a structure whose fixations and bound paths are contrived to neutralize disturbances, but a system set up to maintain typical levels of tension for the tasks typical of the species. It is a practical, active system. And it is set up to do but one task at a time; it is a synthetic whole. Its objectives are external to it; it is bracketed upon a practical field, where a configuration arises in relief against the ground.

In the schema of Lyotard and Deleuze-Guattari, the organism is reactive, a sum of adjustments; it is the orgasmic body that is active, productive. Its excitations produce determinate energy-flows which are segmented and consumed. Yet the actions, the productions are peripheral, not organized synthetically by the postural schema of the whole organism, and they are multiple. The objects with which they are connected are not conceived as objectives, the actions not conceived as purposive, teleological. They are conceived according to the Nietzschean conception of action. For Nietzsche, a living being is a system in which an excess of force is generated; more force issues from it than was transmitted into it, and more force than what is required for its adjustment to its environment. The Apollonian and Dionysian compulsions—compulsion to dream, to produce visions of unreality, and the compulsion to dance, to move in intensive, nonteleological movements—are the Nietzschean names for these productions of an excess, with which Nietzsche identifies life. "I have learned—it is one of my essential steps and advances—to distinguish the driving forces from the directing forces."[1] The directing force—the goals, vocations—are not the origin of the movement. The origin of movement is a quantum of excess force that has to be used up somehow. The directing force is some accident that befalls it from without, extrinsic to the driving force—a match that sets off the keg of powder. The true directing force has to be distinguished from the purpose, the directing force as it is represented in consciousness. The purpose is selected for its beauty and not for its truth. Qua representation it is a production of the Apollonian compulsion. For consciousness is not necessary for life's productions, and is not their efficient cause.

Such is the action of the Deleuze-Guattari molecular desire-machines. They work as couplings with external processes—*which* ones the chance of contiguities determine. They are driven by the compulsion of an excess to flow. They are machines for consummation, for consumption. Every coupling is positive, productive of a flow of force. They do not function for the sake of the maintenance of the organism, and although the active surface is made possible by the reactive organization, the bindings that form the organism do not form for the sake of the production of the excess.

Lyotard and Deleuze-Guattari thus eliminate teleology from the erotogenic body, and from the relationship between the erotogenic body and the organism structure. Also absent from their conception is any species teleology. Libido as Deleuze and Guattari describe it as orphan and celibate. The biological engineering of the genital system and structured species-reproduction never figure in their discussions. The biological fecundity of male and female make up no part of their erotic allure. They in no way connect the particular action, or agitation, the excitations, of libidinal experience with the acts involved in genital reproduction.

> The organized body is the object of reproduction by generation; it is not the subject. The sole subject of reproduction is the unconscious itself, which remains in the circular form of production. Sexuality is not a means at the service of generation; the generation of bodies is at the service of sexuality qua auto-production of the unconscious. Sexuality does not represent a premium for the ego, in exchange for the subordination to the process of generation; on the contrary, generation is the consolation of the ego, its prolongation, the passage from one body to another across which the unconscious only reproduces itself in itself. It is indeed in this sense that we have to say that the unconscious was always an orphan, that it engendered itself in the identity of nature and man, of the world and man.[2]

Only Levinas has connected the orgasmic body with the fecund body. He has done so not through a delineation of the organic, biological processes that could be revealed by objective methods, but through an explication of the inner structure of experience, of the orgasmic experience and of parenthood as an experience. Experience is ex-istence—a movement by which one is thrown out of one's own being toward the other, and by which one is thrown out of one's own state of being toward another being. The libidinal drive conjoins the two in their most extreme form: eroticism is the most total fascination with the alterity of the other; fecundity is one's existence throwing itself out of its own identity, transubstantiation. In the tender and profaning care for the alterity of another there moves a craving of existence to divest itself entirely of its own identity and its own temporality.

This conception emphasizes the existential conception of experience—experience not as representation but as constitutive movement by which a living system is teleologically oriented toward an exterior. The libido, both as orgasmic voluptuousness and as fecundity, is experience in this sense. It is true that this ex-perience also engenders representations that dissimulate it. Levinas's account explains why the other whom this ex-perience aims at is not presented or represented, but it does not explain why the experience then engenders dissimulating erotic phantasms, screen images for unconscious drives. Why does the erotic experience conduct itself in unavowable depths?

Deleuze and Guattari have been instructed not by examining the experience-structure of an erotic excitation, but by examining the production involved in a DNA molecule, which they have used as a model for the "molecular machinery" of desire. Still, their mechanic's analysis has been guided by the Nietzschean interpretation of action, which they have read into the molecular processes. Nietzsche knows that action is positive, is force, inasmuch as it is an inner feeling of exultation, rather than because it is an emanation of externally observable effects. Nietzschean life is at the summit of action in the production of effects that do not exteriorize themselves from it and do not subsist beyond the moment of action: the Apollonian production of phantasms, the Dionysian production of intensive patterns of nonteleological movement. Both Levinas and Deleuze-Guattari have thus presupposed a certain truth, a revealing power, in experience—Levinas in the desire of voluptuousness, taken to reveal the biological aim of fecundity, Deleuze-Guattari in Nietzschean exultation, taken to reveal the molecular processes of desire. They have tacitly made borrowings from what biology, with its specific cognitive methods, sets forth about reproduction, and they find such biological cognition to be in conformity with the cognition credited in voluptuous feeling and parental care, in exultation. What is now required is an epistemological evaluation of the empirical cognition at work in the biology of reproduction, and of the reflection that claims to disengage the truth of erotic experience through the phantasms it engenders.

2. Intentional Libido, Intensive Libido

The phenomenology of the libido interprets it as an intentional structure. Initially, this means that it is not a sum or resultant of processes in the third person, determined by external and internal forces that stimulate them, but a movement determined by its objectives, its future. The libidinal impulse is a teleological or purposive movement, and not a drive or instinct. It is provoked by a meaning, rather than by the physical properties of stimuli.

Sartre interprets its nature in terms of the analysis of lack or want. The libido, qua sexual desire, is an aiming at, a movement determined as a lack of something posited, positive. It is a lack-producing and lack-reproducing process. As such it is pure vacuum, a nothingness of. The movement emptying itself not only determines the objective lacked as lacked, hence as positive; it also posits that object as an object, makes itself consciousness of that object by the distance-producing retreat. This negativist conception of the libido as intentional movement produces conceptual difficulties: what can the libido as craving for self-incarnation be? What can be the reality of the incarnation which Sartre so vividly describes, but which his conceptual opposites reduce to mere appearance? For he describes the subjective form specific to libidinous desire as a desire that sinks back into its own being, is weighted down with itself, desires as substantial hands dragged over flesh, thighs and buttocks pressed against thighs and buttocks.

On the other hand, the negativist interpretation of desire depends on the idea that sexual impulses, qua desire, are want and lack. Lyotard and Deleuze-Guattari contest this: for them sexual excitations are positive, force, production, the craving of an excess to discharge itself. If nothing is obtained through all the orgasmic grapplings, seizings, and penetratings, this would not be, as in Sartre's interpretation, because the impassioned orgasm loses sight of its objective, but because, as Freud said, the pleasure consists in the release and discharge of swollen quanta of excitation.

Merleau-Ponty preserves, from the intentional idea, the notion that the libidinal behaviors are determined by meanings and not by material properties of stimuli, and that they are teleologically oriented beyond oneself, upon a mundane figure. But for him this self-organizing arc is the mobilizing axis of the body, and not a nihilating movement of consciousness that departs from the being of the body. What can transcend itself, its here-now, is being, and precisely sensible being, despite all the weight of tradition that defines it by inherence in a here-now. It is the body qua sensible being that orients itself in a mobile way in behaviors directed to external objectives, makes the exteriority into object-objectives. The reality of the libido is not mental, not seated in the mental space of an unconsciousness; it is physical, corporeal, it is the organizing axis of the agent body. The libido is seated in the body's sensibility, it is sensible consciousness; the unconscious is structured with body motility. The unconscious, theater of representations of libidinal aims and objectives, is the sensibility of the body.

Levinas has retained, from the original concept of intentionality, not so much the character of object-objective determined, as the character of a movement out of one's being to alterity. Ex-istence, ex-perience, is for him not so much consciousness, self-consciousness, but fascination with alterity. It is not so much teleological or purposive, where the attainment of the objective is appropriation and self-consolidation; it is more fundamentally expenditure at a loss, self-evacuation. The paradigm in his thinking is not, as for Merleau-Ponty, a movement, a gesture, but sensibility qua exposure. Whereas Merleau-Ponty everywhere reinterprets sensibility as *prise*, prehension, motility, Levinas sees it as exposedness, susceptibility. Not the tropism of a substance putting out feelers to draw the outside into itself, but the tropism of a full sufficient substance gratuitously exposing itself to the exterior, to wounds and outrage. Orgasm would not be the intensification of violence, penetration, seizure, manipulation, that Sartre saw, but a process of striated muscles turning into glands, inner surfaces or orifices turning into mucous membrane, a body turning inside out through all its orifices. The orgasmic body would be a body seeking ever more susceptibility, exposing itself to torment and dependence, exposing its very identity.

Lyotard and Deleuze-Guattari do not see in eroticism the waste and superabundance by which a species ensures the maintenance of its species type despite its realization in individuals with a compulsion to self-preservation. In their conception, the excess or discharge is the essential; the libidinal drive is the opposite of any intentional and teleological aim.

Plato already had seen in eros an excess over and beyond the biological finalities, but he made it transcendence in general, the force by which life seeks ever more extensive, more comprehensive ends, and finally beauty and immortality, immortal beauty, the splendor of the unending. The surplus force produced over and beyond the biological finality would retain the teleological form; it would have within itself the power to posit new, unnatural ends, and finally to posit the unending as the ultimate telos or horizon of universal teleology. Thus its energies, diverted into the purposes of civilization, make all energies teleological. For Freud, too, the surplus which all civilization employs in its works is the excess of the original vital aim—an excess produced by the inhibition of that aim. The specifically purposive character of the energies employed in civilization derives from the purposiveness of libido. Not, as in Plato, that they derive the general form of purposiveness from it, but that they must always represent new purposes to mask the vital objective. All the goals of civilization lure by virtue of being phallic metaphors. In them libido seeks in devious, disguised forms its original and natural end, immediate gratification.

What is new in Lyotard and Deleuze-Guattari is the Nietzschean doctrine conceiving of life without any intrinsic teleology. For Nietzsche, a species does not have its own specific form of structure as its telos. Nietzsche identifies the inner sensation of life with exultation and not with contentment—life is the feeling of gratuitously expanding force within, not the feeling of the filling of a hunger, an emptiness being compensated for with a content. All the reactive structures, which make adjustment to the environment possible, are in an organism at the service of active forces. In the evolution of a species an organ comes into being accidentally—it is randomness caught on the wing—and then gets utilized by the dominant will in that organism, utilized most likely in quite different ways at different times.[3] The intrinsic organic structure is neither its own telos, nor is it assembled by some teleology.

To Lyotard and Deleuze-Guattari the libidinal appears as the production of excess, superfluity, that energizes the surfaces of all the practical, intellectual, social, and aesthetic organisms of civilization, without continuing the biological aim. The libidinal impulse is not straightforward and univocal, like an intentionality, but is always ambivalent, a vertigo following an aimless spiral of phantasms or juncture of incompossibles. The representations that swarm about the libidinal impulses, no longer their final causes, become their after-effects, their dissolute creations. The word *creation* need not be taken too seriously: these representations enshrine no revelation and monumentalize nothing. To designate them as false is already to look at them in the spirit of seriousness. And erotic phantasms are not individual myths in which, if not truth, then meaning, life-ordaining meaning, would be elaborated. They are signs no more than are the wanton colors in the orifices of Caucasian, Semitic, or African bodies signs. Nietzsche conceived the representations of the will as products of a compulsive artistry; but they are, according to him, not only symptoms of the force of the will but also necessary for its discharge. They contract the will into a perspective. Nietzsche uses here in a new way the ancient idea that representations are forms, formative as well as informative. Doubtless the erotic phantasms do not form perspectives as Kantian schemata of the imagination. They do not inform but deform a sensuous diversity and deform the will too, if it is true that the libidinal impulse begins, as Freud declared, by an anaclitic deviation or perversion of the organ function.

3. The Directions of Erotic Sense

There is something like an erotic sense—a coherence of libidinal configurations and erotic adventures. A life *makes* sense, Merleau-Ponty put it, intentionally extending itself in space and in time across the intentional arc of the libido which fixes an organism on another organism and on the flesh of the world. A life contracts death already and birth still in the spasms of the orgasmic chiasm. Through its libidinal encounters and mischances, adventures and defeats, a life assembles chance events into the configuration of a destiny, makes gratuitous touches and nonsensical bouts of laughter necessary to itself, links up mute and anonymous corners of the historical landscape into the web of an erotic enchantment, makes comedy or tragedy or farce out of reflex arcs, secretions, orgasms, and sleep. The libidinal agitation, the intentional appropriation it realizes, make the public functions I

fulfill and the universally significant and verifiable words I
utter convey the singular purport of my personal destiny,
borne by a passion which is as anonymous as flesh and nature.

What does *sense* mean here? Sense, in an erotically
charged body, is not something ideal, not an intemporal invariant which I think of and constitute; it is the way each
sensuous aspect and tone of that body flows into the next, in a
sort of "transitional synthesis," and composes a charged
configuration that refers immediately to the genital powers of
my body. Merleau-Ponty worked to shift phenomenology's
analysis of sense out of the framework of the Husserlian opposition of reality and ideality—where meaning is conceived as
the selfsameness of traits across space and time. Sense is
rather to be understood as a Gestalt—properties that are perceptible, like the properties of the component elements, but
belong to the structure as such. For Merleau-Ponty sense does
mean synthesis, a whole, a unity in the future toward which
an intentional movement advances and which it describes in
its movement. This concept of sense is bound up with the
notion of intentionality.

Merleau-Ponty finds sense in logos, in assembling; it is the
comprehensive factor which is comprehended. Lyotard, on
the contrary, understands what is significant to be the *figure*
that articulates. His *Discours, figure*[4] draws attention to the
letters in discourse as broken partial objects, to the words as
undecomposable blocks, undivided fluxes or full bodies with
a tonic value. These belong to the order of breaths, sighs, cries,
aspirations of desire. Similarly, in the plastic arts, he considers
the figure to be formed by the active line, the multidimen-
sional point, and the multiple configurations to be formed by
the passive line and the surface it engenders. In dreams, what
works in dream-work is not the meaning, but a figural element
arousing configurations of images that use and incorporate
words, make them flow, make them follow fluxes and elements
that are not linguistic. Meaning-elements are in dream-work
treated like things, linked up in chains and collages of images.
These "figures," distinguished from significant *Gestalten* or
meanings, are the aesthetic element, but Lyotard immediately
links them to the unconscious and the primary process. In
Economie libidinale the intensities flow, depart, flee, forming

not paths and perspectives but labyrinths, forming a space without terms and without termination—forming not synthetic identities but figures. The properties of such figures would have to be worked out in conjunction with a study of primary-process art, and not classical representational or significant arts. Pop art, happenings, the music of John Cage, would be material out of which a grammar of the libidinal sense would have to be extracted.

The concept of *code* governs Deleuze and Guattari's treatment of the erotic sense. Every machine is coded; it functions only if it determines for itself what flux to draw off? Where? How and with what stroke? What place to leave to other producers or antiproducers? Or is one to choke on what one devours, swallow air, shit with one's mouth?[5] Conjunctions, connections are made on the surface of inscription, on the body without organs, by the attraction and repulsion of the multiplicity of the coded molecular processes. Thus chains are formed where codes are coupled and connected, disjoined and detached.

All repression can be described as forcing the desire-machines to function according to a linear and univocal coding. For desire-machines, in the measure that they are productive, form fragmentary, polyvocal chains, less a language than a jargon, continually elaborated with all sorts of heterogeneous elements. There is no underlying plan; the connections are made on the recording surface by chance collisions and repulsions. There is no negative in the unconscious, no force of exclusion; the exclusions come only from the play of inhibitors and repressors that make the desire-machinery into a species-identifiable type. The chains of the unconscious are not propositions. The connections are by passive and not active, intentional, synthesis. They are anagrams, patchworks, collages, works of *bricolage*.

Deleuze and Guattari have taken from Proust the idea of a noncomprehensive, non-Gestaltist whole, a whole that is added to the chain as another part. In the course of a work of literature the perspectives converge from time to time, overlap or dovetail, and something like unity, a whole, takes form. Still, it is but another episode in the prolongation of the narrative; it is neither a moment when, in a kind of retrospective intuition, the constitutive origin of the events is revealed, nor a moment when they culminate in a final integration. Because this moment of summation took form, the next local episode will be affected and will affect it too; the whole becomes another episode affecting the turn the narrative takes. And it has a retroactive effect on all the events, views and perspectives elaborated thus far; the moment when the whole structure emerges throws a new light on them, and this light is but another perspective on those perspectives. (We have seen how Deleuze and Guattari apply this conception to the relationship between the desire-machines and the body without organs: the body without organs is a whole, but a whole alongside of them which repels them as it supports them.)

Thus there is not one intentional arc, consubstantial with the identity of a life, which synthesizes all the episodes of the libidinal drive, all the impulses, and is immanent in them—or rather there *are* such moments of synthesis, totalization, essence and destiny revealed in a moment, in an adventure, but they are episodes among others.

These theories—of the figural in Lyotard, of the codes of the unconscious in Deleuze and Guattari—we find inchoate and undeveloped in their work. We cannot complain that we are still lacking the specific grammars and rules of syntax for them. We can form our best notions of them by practicing the interpretation of dreams with Freud and Lacan (the basic text, Deleuze and Guattari write, being "The Purloined Letter"[6]), by making sense out of the schizophrenic chains of Beckett and Artaud.

Lyotard's concept of figure and Deleuze-Guattari's concept of code convey only an informative dimension of sense—informative yet not indicative, sense as determining an articulation, not as revealing something beyond itself. Levinas alone has outlined a nascent theory of the vocative and imperative sense of the erotic solicitation. We require a concept of provocative sense, a semantics of the secrecy that is not disclosed but profaned. We require a semiotics of the imperative force of the erotic. There is, in all the authors we have studied, including Levinas, no concept of the imperative, ordering sense of eros that is at work where an erotic sense is found embedded in geometrical reason, in architectonics, political economics, the destiny of a state, and the sense of the sacred, that which was at work in the erotic civilization of Khajuraho in medieval India.[7]

4. *The Erotic Deviation*

Completely absent in Lyotard and in Deleuze-Guattari is any sense of contact with an alien passion, which makes voluptuousness that paralyzed fixation on some familiar anatomic detail as though it contained the memory of abysses, that stupefied conviction that what a lover is obsessed with is, even after all these loves and all these orgasms since first *Homo habilis* first touched with the touch of affection, as yet unrevealed.

The reduction of the post-Oedipal forms of person, of the genital forms of the human, of the phallic forms of subjectivity—shown to be phantasms, products of repression, and not the primary excitants of libido—does not abolish this alterity from the structure of eros. For to polarize libido as desire for a male, a female, a human being, a person, or a subjectivity is but to polarize it on a complementarity, a divergency, and not an alterity. Is there not an *ecstatic* structure to the molecular processes themselves? Is there not an *alterity* toward which the intensities flow?

The libido is passionate; it is not an operation that initiates itself. Levinas has accounted for this passionate nature of libidinal impulses by constructing a concept of alterity different from any concept of person or subjectivity. The alterity in the other that excites the voluptuous passion is not a molar and statistical whole, is not the bearer of the traits that determine masculinity, femininity, or humanity. The other is a singular— without concept, without predicates.

Such alterity is not made of divergence, difference, distance, or absence. It is not made of the structuring and distributive instance of law, nor of a phallic ideal or value. It is the incompossible with which contact is made in the libidinal intensity; it remains an impossible that one cannot apprehend, that oppresses or obsesses. It is that with which contact has already been made, that with which processes and fluxes find themselves already coupled and connected, as in a predestination. It is what afflicts and what quickens in the hand that passes over you, in the womb that closes against you and over you, in the skin, all exposed, reversing into its orifices yet still everywhere surface, across which residual fluxes, *voluptas*, torments of pleasure, are consumed. It will have to be described in terms other than those of subjectivity, structure, personage, or even entity.

Notes

The English wording of translated citations has been occasionally amended.

1. Freedom and Slavery in Sexuality

1. Jean-Paul Sartre, "Faces," trans. Anne P. Jones in Maurice Natanson, ed., *Essays in Phenomenology* (The Hague: Martinus Nijhoff, 1966), pp. 160–61.

2. Jean-Paul Sartre, *Outline of a Theory of the Emotions*, trans. Bernard Frechtman (New York: Philosophical Library, 1948), p. 84.

3. Jean-Paul Sartre, *Being and Nothingness*, trans. Hazel E. Barnes (New York: Washington Square Press, 1956), p. 393.

4. Ibid., p. 394.

5. Maurice Merleau-Ponty, *Phenomenology of Perception*, trans. Colin Smith (London: Routledge & Kegan Paul, 1962), p. 356; *Signs*, trans. Richard C. McCleary (Evanston: Northwestern University Press, 1964), pp. 15–16, 169; *The Visible and the Invisible*, trans. Alphonso F. Lingis (Evanston: Northwestern University Press, 1968), pp. 13–14.

6. Sartre therefore holds to a theory of the seductive and not pragmatic essence of language. Nietzsche did also, when he derived human speech from the vocalisms of lower animals, insects, and birds, where the vocalism functions for seduction and not for the communication of food and danger signals. Cf. *Thus Spoke Zarathustra*, trans. Walter Kaufmann (New York: Penguin, 1978), p. 217.

7. Jean-Paul Sartre, *Being and Nothingness*, p. 451. "What for the Other is his *taste of himself* becomes for me the *Other's flesh*. The flesh is the pure contingency of presence. It is ordinarily hidden by clothes, make-up, the cut of the hair or beard, the expression, etc. But in the course of long acquaintance with a person there always comes an instant when all these disguises are thrown off and when I find myself in the presence of the pure *contingency of his presence*. In this case I achieve in the face or the other parts of a body the pure intuition of the flesh. This intuition is not only knowledge; it is the affective apprehension of an absolute contingency, and this apprehension is a particular type of *nausea*."

8. Ibid., pp. 218–19.

9. Ibid., p. 290.

10. It is true that at the end of his book Sartre recognizes the need to work out a phenomenology of action in quite different terms. The efficacy of conscious action—it affects the very being and not only the phenomenal discriminations of things—makes it necessary to conceive the active subject

in terms no longer of pure distancing from being, but of a sort of synthetic—Gestaltist—compound of intentionality and exterior substantiality (ibid., p. 795).

11. Ibid., p. 781.

12. Ibid., pp. 781–82.

13. Ibid., p. 517.

14. Ibid., pp. 455–57.

15. As Nietzsche said, man does not aim to attain to pleasure and avoid pain (only the Englishman does); man, the most courageous animal, suffers more than any other animal, continually invents sufferings for himself, seeks out suffering, provided he can give it a meaning. *On the Genealogy of Morals*, trans. Walter Kaufmann (New York: Vintage, 1969), p. 162.

16. Jean-Paul Sartre, *Being and Nothingness*, p. 142.

17. Ibid., p. 797.

18. Ibid., p. 798.

19. Ibid., p. 747.

20. Ibid., p. 798.

2. Sense and Non-sense in Sexuality

1. Kurt Goldstein, *The Organism*, no translator given (Boston: Beacon Press, 1963). Paul Schilder, *The Image & Appearance of the Human Body* (New York: Science Editions, 1950).

2. Maurice Merleau-Ponty, *Signs*, trans. Richard C. McCleary (Evanston: Northwestern University Press, 1964), p. 15.

3. Maurice Merleau-Ponty, *Phenomenology of Perception*, trans. Colin Smith (London: Routledge & Kegan Paul, 1962), p. 4.

4. Maurice Merleau-Ponty, *The Visible and the Invisible*, trans. Alphonso F. Lingis (Evanston: Northwestern University Press, 1968), p. 135.

5. Maurice Merleau-Ponty, *Phenomenology of Perception*, p. 167.

6. Maurice Merleau-Ponty, *Themes from the Lectures*, trans. John O'Neill (Evanston: Northwestern University Press, 1970), p. 129.

7. Maurice Merleau-Ponty, *Signs*, p. 175.

8. Maurice Merleau-Ponty, *Phenomenology of Perception*, p. 154.

3. Phenomenology of the Face and Carnal Intimacy

1. Emmanuel Levinas, *Totality and Infinity*, trans. Alphonso Lingis (Pittsburgh: Duquesne University Press and The Hague: Martinus Nijhoff, 1969), pp. 75, 197–201.

2. Maurice Merleau-Ponty, *The Visible and the Invisible*, trans. Alphonso Lingis (Evanston: Northwestern University Press, 1968), p. 135.

3. Emmanuel Levinas, *Totality and Infinity*, pp. 263–64.

4. Martin Heidegger, *Being and Time*, trans. John Macquarrie and Edward Robinson (New York and Evanston: Harper & Row, 1962), pp. 235–41.

5. Emmanuel Levinas, *Totality and Infinity*, pp. 256–57.

6. Ibid. Also Emmanuel Levinas, "Langage et proximité," in *En découv-*

rant l'existence avec Husserl et Heidegger, 2nd ed. (Paris: Vrin, 1967), pp. 227–28.

7. Emmanuel Levinas, Totality and Infinity, pp. 264–65.

8. Ibid., pp. 263–65.

Capitalisme et schizophrénie, tome I, L'Anti-Oedipe (Paris: Minuit, 1972).

9. Ibid., p. 264.

10. Ibid., p. 267.

11. Ibid., pp. 282–83. Cf. Emmanuel Levinas, Existence and Existents, trans. Alphonso Lingis (The Hague: Martinus Nijhoff, 1978), pp. 91–92.

12. Max Scheler, The Nature of Sympathy (Hamden: Archon, 1970), pp. 166–68.

13. Emmanuel Levinas, "La trace de l'autre," in En découvrant l'existence avec Husserl et Heidegger, pp. 197–202.

4. The Intensive Zone

1. Sigmund Freud, Beyond the Pleasure Principle, trans. James Strachey, Standard Edition, Vol. XVIII (London: Hogarth Press, 1955), p. 7.

2. Ibid., p. 28.

3. Ibid., p. 62.

4. Ibid., p. 26.

5. Daniel Paul Schreber, Memoirs of My Nervous Illness, trans. Ida Macalpine and Richard A. Hunter (London: Wm. Dawson & Sons, 1955).

6. Ibid., p. 178.

7. Jean-François Lyotard, Economie libidinale (Paris: Minuit, 1974), p. 76.

8. Ibid., pp. 20–21.

9. Ibid., p. 79.

10. Ibid., p. 304.

11. Ibid., p. 304.

5. The Carnal Machinery

1. Michel Foucault, Madness and Civilization: A History of Insanity in the Age of Reason, trans. Richard Howard (New York: Random House, 1971).

2. Gilles Deleuze and Félix Guattari, Anti-Oedipus, trans. Robert Hurley, Mark Seem, and Helen R. Lane (New York: Viking, 1977), p. 50.

3. Ibid., p. 294.

4. Ibid.

5. Samuel Butler, Erewhon (New York: E. P. Dutton, 1965).

6. Jacques Monod, Chance and Necessity, trans. Austryn Wainhouse (New York: Knopf, 1971), p. 98.

7. Ibid.

8. Gilles Deleuze, Logique du sens (Paris: Minuit, 1969), pp. 217–27.

9. Deleuze and Guattari, Anti-Oedipus, p. 4.

10. Sigmund Freud, Psycho-Analytic Notes on an Autobiographical Account of a Case of Paranoia, trans. James Strachey, Standard Edition, Vol. XII (London: Hogarth Press, 1958), p. 17.

11. Michel Carrouges, Les machines célibataires (Paris: Arcanes, 1954).

12. Kurt Goldstein, *The Organism* (Boston: Beacon Press, 1963).

13. Deleuze and Guattari, *Anti-Oedipus*, p. 18.

14. Ibid., p. 131.

15. Friedrich Nietzsche, *The Portable Nietzsche*, trans. Walter Kaufmann (New York: Penguin, 1976), pp. 685–86.

16. Deleuze and Guattari, *Anti-Oedipus*, p. 35.

6. *Libido and Alterity*

1. Friedrich Nietzsche, *The Gay Science*, trans. Walter Kaufmann (New York: Vintage, 1974), p. 315.

2. Gilles Deleuze and Félix Guattari, *Anti-Oedipus*, trans. Robert Hurley, Mark Seem, and Helen R. Lane (New York: Viking, 1977), p. 108.

3. Friedrich Nietzsche, *On the Genealogy of Morals*, trans. Walter Kaufmann (New York: Vintage, 1969), pp. 77–78.

4. Jean-François Lyotard, *Discours, figure* (Paris: Klincksieck, 1974).

5. Deleuze and Guattari, *Anti-Oedipus*, p. 38.

6. Jacques Lacan, *Ecrits* (Paris: Seuil, 1966), "Le séminaire sur 'La Lettre volée,'" pp. 11–61.

7. Alphonso Lingis, *Excesses* (New York: State University of New York Press, 1984), Ch. IV, "Khajuraho."

Selective Bibliography

Jean-Paul Sartre (1905–1980)

Esquisse d'une théorie des émotions (Paris: Hermann, 1939). Translated by Bernard Frechtman: *The Emotions: Outline of a Theory* (New York: Philosophical Library, 1948) and by Philip Mairet: *Sketch for a Theory of the Emotions* (London: Methuen, 1962).

L'être et le néant: Essai d'ontologie phénoménologique (Paris: Gallimard, 1943). Translated by Hazel E. Barnes: *Being and Nothingness* (New York: Washington Square Press, 1956).

L'idiot de la famille, 3 vols. (Paris: Gallimard, 1971). Translated by Carol Cosman (Chicago: University of Chicago Press, 1981), Vol. I.

Saint Genet, comédien et martyr (Paris: Gallimard, 1952). Translated by Bernard Frechtman: *Saint Genet, Actor and Martyr* (New York: Braziller, 1963).

Maurice Merleau-Ponty (1907–1961)

Maurice Merleau-Ponty à la Sorbonne (Paris: *Bulletin de Psychologie*, n. 236, tome XVIII, 3–6, novembre 1964). "Les relations avec autrui chez l'enfant" was translated by William Cobb in James M. Edie, ed., *The Primacy of Perception*, (Evanston: Northwestern University Press, 1964).

Phénoménologie de la perception (Paris: Gallimard, 1945). Translated by Colin Smith: *Phenomenology of Perception* (London: Routledge & Kegan Paul, 1962).

Résume de cours, Collège de France 1952–1960 (Paris: Gallimard, 1968). Translated by John O'Neill: *Themes from the Lectures at the Collège de France 1952–1960* (Evanston: Northwestern University Press, 1970).

Signes (Paris: Gallimard, 1960). Translated by Richard C. McCleary: *Signs* (Evanston: Northwestern University Press, 1964).

Le visible et l'invisible (Paris: Gallimard, 1964). Translated by Alphonso Lingis: *The Visible and the Invisible* (Evanston: Northwestern University Press, 1968).

Emmanuel Levinas (b. 1906)

Autrement qu'être ou au-delà de l'essence (La Haye: Martinus Nijhoff, 1974). Translated by Alphonso Lingis: *Otherwise than Being, or Beyond Essence* (The Hague, Boston, London: Martinus Nijhoff, 1981).

De l'existence à l'existant (Paris: Fontaine, 1947). Second edition (Paris:

Vrin, 1978). Translated by Alphonso Lingis, *Existence and Existents* (The Hague: Martinus Nijhoff, 1978).

En découvrant l'existence avec Husserl et Heidegger (Paris: Vrin, 1967).

Totalité et Infini, Essai sur l'extériorité (La Haye: Martinus Nijhoff, 1961). Translated by Alphonso Lingis: *Totality and Infinity: An Essay on Exteriority* (Pittsburgh: Duquesne University Press; The Hague: Martinus Nijhoff, 1969).

Jean-François Lyotard (b. 1924)

Le différend (Paris: Minuit, 1983).

Dérive à partir de Marx et Freud (Paris: Union Générale d'Editions, 1973).

Discours, figure (Paris: Klinksieck, 1974).

Des dispositifs puslionnels (Paris: Union Générale d'Editions, 1973).

Economie libidinale (Paris: Minuit, 1974).

Gilles Deleuze and Félix Guattari

Capitalisme et schizophrénie, tôme I, L'Anti-Oedipe (Paris: Minuit, 1972). Translated by Robert Hurley, Mark Seem, and Helen R. Lane: *Anti-Oedipus, Capitalism and Schizophrenia* (New York: Viking Press, 1977).

Capitalisme et schizophrénie, tôme II, Mille Plateaux (Paris: Minuit, 1980).

Gilles Deleuze

Dialogues, en collaboration avec Claire Parnet (Paris: Flammarion, 1977).

Différence et répétition (Paris: Presses Universitaires de France, 1968).

Logique du sens (Paris: Minuit, 1969).

Présentation de Sacher Masoch (Paris: Minuit, 1967).

Rhizome-Introduction (Paris: Minuit, 1976).

Félix Guattari

L'inconscient machinique (Paris: Editions Recherches, 1979).

Psychanalyse et transversalité (Paris: Maspero, 1972).

La révolution moléculaire (Paris: Editions Recherches, 1977).

Index

127